BRITAIN IN OLD PHOTOGRAPHS

NORTHAMPTON

ROBERT COOK

SUTTON PUBLISHING LIMITED

Sutton Publishing Limited
Phoenix Mill · Thrupp · Stroud
Gloucestershire · GL5 2BU

First published 1996

Cover photographs: (front) making shell cases
at the Express Lift Co.'s Abbey Works in
Weedon Road during the First World War;
(back) volunteers for the Northamptonshire
Yeomanry during the First World War.

Title page photograph: A magnificent
steamroller, built in 1899 and restored by
Bert Henman of the Borough Engineers' Dept,
leading the Carnival parade, 17 June 1971.
(Northampton Borough Council)

British Library Cataloguing in Publication Data
A catalogue record for this book is available from the
British Library.

ISBN 0-7509-1318-5

Typeset in 10/12 Perpetua.
Typesetting and origination by
Sutton Publishing Limited.
Printed in Great Britain by
Ebenezer Baylis, Worcester.

The Drapery looking north in 1971, with traffic flowing easily around the new one-way system.
(Northampton Borough Council)

CONTENTS

The old fountain, Market Square, 17 April 1962. Erected in 1863, it marked the marriage of the Prince of Wales to Princess Alexandra of Denmark and it was presented to the town by Captain Isaacs, CO of the 5th Corps Northampton Volunteers. Deemed unsafe, it was demolished soon after this picture was taken. (Northampton Borough Council)

INTRODUCTION

I was born and brought up about twenty miles south of Northampton, and the first I knew of the place was as a small boy struggling to read its long name on the destination blinds of service 346 United Counties buses heading that way through my home town of Winslow. Not until the mid-1960s did my widowed mother take us on an expensive jaunt to see what Northampton actually looked like. Lucky for me I saw it before the big changes that were afoot. Humans cannot leave things as they are. It is in their nature, especially the wealthy and young, to imagine gains from change. Ever since Neolithic man arrived in Britain, the original wildwood and all it contained has been on the wane. How easy to see faults only among the Brazilians who now devastate rainforests. They are only doing what our ancestors did earlier to accommodate the insatiable demands and spread of humanity.

Northampton itself is first mentioned in 1086. The Conqueror's son, William Rufus, granted Northampton – the north Homestead or Home Farm – as a mesne borough to Simon de Senlis who married William's niece, Matilda. Simon built the castle, enlarged the town defences and established the nunnery at Delapre Abbey. By 1189 there were 300 houses, the town's growth encouraged by its profitable position in the Nene Valley at the convergence of trade routes. In the same year Richard I granted the town's Charter in return for money for the third Crusade. The Charter was a generous one; it gave the townsfolk the right to elect their own reeve (whose title changed to mayor in 1215), and to collect their own taxes free from outside claims, and granted them the same rights and privileges as those of the City of London.

Relations with royalty fluctuated. The town prospered from the wool and cloth industry and gained a university. This development offered rich pickings in the age where brute force could secure advantage. Local barons, supported by students, rebelled against the king in 1264 but the town's monks, then a political breed, undermined the defences and let in the royal force. Pardoned four years later, the town was never quite trusted and rightly so, for it again turned against the king during the English Civil War. Its disloyalty was not wholly unforgiven, however. When most of the town was razed by fire in 1675 after a woman set alight her thatched roof, the king offered succour and a reduction in taxes. The fire was a blessing in disguise – in 1724

Daniel Defoe described the rebuilt town as 'the handsomest town in all this part of England . . . finely rebuilt with brick and stone and the streets spacious and wide'.

The common people have suffered over the years. Trade made Northampton a thoroughfare and so brought plague – the 'beggars' disease'. The Industrial Revolution accelerated the growth of local industries, especially shoe-making, using hides from local animals. By 1712 the town's population was almost five thousand, most of whom were engaged in shoe-making and hosiery. London's shoe firms were attracted to the town by the comparatively low wages, and the nineteenth century saw factories and terraces of tiny houses unfold across the eastern landscape, giving birth to a new working-class subculture. Nowadays cheap labour working abroad threatens the home footwear industry with extinction.

The two World Wars had massive economic and social impact locally, while the inter-war years created new hardship, but the post-war period offered new prosperity. The effect of this on Northampton was powerfully analysed by Jeremy Seabrook, himself descended from local shoemakers, in *The Everlasting Feast* (Penguin, 1974). Returning to the town for a while, he recalled the opportunities offered by Northampton Grammar School for pupils who passed the eleven plus to leave the poverty subculture: 'We met in the no-man's-land of those who have rejected their social formation. Our teachers – who seemed to live on a single estate constructed during the 1930s and were consumed with nostalgia for an anti-urban medievalism that strung chains of timbered, gabled homesteads around the town – failed to present us with any good reason for a commitment to any social or intellectual values.'

But the engine of advancement had no need of intellectuals. Leather-based industries welcomed the youth fashion market that was then exploding. Some young professional newcomers perhaps saw themselves as superior, but Seabrook was sceptical, watching them passing through: 'For the first month or two the new job and the new friends are enough to keep them involved, arguing with prissy headmistresses about the kind of garment in which it is suitable to instruct the young.'

Image is everything today. The 1966 expansion plan glittered, and seeds of newness broke out like beanstalks, cracking pavements and shaking old buildings, quickly maturing into vast edifices with lifts and stairways. Of course there were cynics and old stagers who kept harking back to 'better times'. These fundamental changes did not make national headlines; the town simply developed and expanded. I am attracted to Seabrook's view: 'During 1971 and 1972, the expansion of Northampton became for me a symbol of the new culture, tyrannical and inexorable in its compulsions . . . a more subtle and less readily discernible bondage.' This may be true, but most people prefer to believe that all change brings freedom – there are new opportunities on offer like the Millennium development and the fairground museum to keep the party going.

Robert Cook, 1996

IT'S ONLY NATURAL

Cllr Alwyn Hargreaves is among those enjoying all the fun of the merry-go-round at St Crispin's Fair in 1994. (G. White)

All Saints' Church, *c.* 1903. The building incorporates a statue of King Charles II who gave the town a thousand tons of timber for rebuilding after the great fire of 1675 and halved the town's taxes for a year. But after the town's disloyalty in the Civil War, the king had already done much to punish the town, ordering the castle walls and town defences to be destroyed. All Saints' Church was also the place where Henry I gathered the English barons and forced them to support his daughter's claim to the throne. The town's first one-way traffic system went around All Saints Square, where PC Harry Powell did point duty. His nephew Baden recalls: 'He had a voice like a fog-horn. One blast from it would stop the car, let alone the fella in it.' (J. Ounsworth)

Castle Ashby, *c*. 1907. A few miles east of Northampton, off the Bedford Road, Castle Ashby was the home of the Compton family, a key force in local politics until the Spencers got the better of them. In modern times the Spencers have become a household name. As long ago as 1920 F.W. Crose was holding speed trials for his 125cc Skootamota (which sounds surprisingly Japanese) on Castle Ashby's drive, reaching the hideously fast average speed of 19.5 mph. (J. Ounsworth)

Harry Smith, a keen cinema-goer in the 1920s, recalls the Savoy cinema at the bottom of The Mounts: 'Harold Nash played the organ and was known nationally. His organ used to come up out of the floor and everybody waited to have a singsong. John Walker, pictured here at Turners Musical Merry-Go-Round, recaptured a bit of that old nostalgia in 1984. John said: 'People were sceptical when Nigel Turner opened the place at Wootton. It looked like a big barn from the outside, but it was a great success. I enjoyed my time working there.' Jean Wooding recalls another musical age, the 1950s: 'I used to follow all the local Northampton bands. The only way you could see them out of town was by getting a ride on their coach. There were dance halls all over the place. You could write a book about our exploits with the bands. We had big bands like Ted Heath's. When they came you just stood and watched them, entranced.' Jean married local bandleader Jimmy Wooding. (John Walker)

The first Northampton Town Football Club, who achieved fourth place in the league of 1897/8. Back row, left to right: B. Smith, W.J. Westmorland (chairman), A.J. Darnell (vice-president), J. Whiting, J. Sargent, C. Gyde (treasurer), A. Jones (secretary), A. Dunkley. Front row: C. Baker, C. Remmett, T. Litchfield. Westmorland, Darnell and Jones all went on to become key figures in the Northants Football Association. (Northants Football Association)

Excelsior Amateur Athletic Club, c. 1920. Running was a cheap sport and popular with working men. Prizes could be won at local sports days and Timkens sports ground was a popular place in recent years. (G. White)

This is young Nellie Abbey of Stantonbury on her way to Northampton for a fancy dress parade to raise money for a hospital in Newport Pagnell. She recalled: 'My bike was covered with imitation grapes. I made hundreds of them from dark blue crepe paper stuffed with wadding. The leaves came from a vine in the garden.' Bicycles offered freedom as well as a means of transport. Freedom and flowers were once again the order of the day in 1989 when Northampton celebrated its Charter of Freedom 'bought' 800 years earlier from King Richard I who needed money for armies. When the Earl of Northampton died, without heir, in 1184, the townsfolk seized their chance to negotiate freedoms that few other English folk had. There were more celebrations in June 1989 when Prince Charles and Princess Diana opened the celebratory flower festival at the church of the Holy Sepulchre. (B. Powell)

These locals with the pub landlord make a forlorn sight outside the Gasometer pub at the junction of Gas Street and Horseshoe Street in about 1920. The war had just finished, jobs were scarce and men tramped miles to find them, frequently taking refuge in the workhouse. Beer drinking offered some comfort. The *Northampton Mercury* reported on late nineteenth-century workmen thus: 'Possessing health and industry, the wages of a married labourer will sustain him in comparative comfort, until a rising offspring shall awaken him to a sense of difficulty and embarrassment . . . the last spark of shame extinguished, he heartily joins in "hang sorrow and drive away care, the Parish is sure to find us".' Gordon White observed: 'They used to say there was only one town comparable for pubs and that was Great Yarmouth, where most Northampton folk went for their holidays.' The area shown here was demolished and replaced by St Peter's Way, perhaps so-named to suggest that it was ordained by the Almighty. (G. White)

The coronation celebrations for George V in the town centre in 1910. King George was a keen imperialist and happily abandoned all his German titles to establish his line as the House of Windsor. The townsfolk always loved a bit of pageantry but did their bit to stay the hand of absolute royal power. William I recognized the town's strategic importance and Norman earls surrounded it with stout walls, adding magnificent churches like the Holy Sepulchre and All Saints. Simon de Montfort and the free citizens rose against King John but failed to hold the castle against the Royal forces who were aided by treacherous monks. But over the years, kings began listening more to common people, and there was stability and prosperity, especially after the Civil War. (G. White)

Laura Sargent at Beckett and Sarjant School in Kingswell Street. She is wearing a gilded oak apple brooch, commemorating Charles II's gift of timber to the town after the great fire of 1675; Charles II, of course, had hidden in an oak tree to escape his pursuers. (G. White)

Thomas Sargent, who was born just over the border in Turvey, Bedfordshire, in 1851. His father was a farm worker and he had little education. His grandson Gordon White said: 'There was no such thing as childhood then. Tom learned shoe-making at Olney and walked to Northampton to get a job. There he met my gran, Caroline Coleman. They married at St Edmund's Church. He's pictured here in the uniform of The Volunteers, a force similar to the Territorial Army. They had to buy their own uniforms, which were grey with mauve facings.' (G. White)

Rose Sargent looks rather frail in this formal pose, taken early this century. One of the factory poor, she lost four sons from TB before contracting it herself and dying. In those days childbirth itself was dangerous, but large families were common for many reasons, including the hope that there would be at least one surviving child to look after the parents in their old age. (G. White)

Short skirts arrived in the 1920s, along with the vote for women and 'flappers'. Women's Lib has been advancing ever since. This is Suzanne Rollestone in the summer of 1966 at the family's chalet near the present Billing Aquadrome. Suzanne said: 'There were about forty chalets and we had a caravan there. It was a good place to get away from our newsagent and post office in Marefair, where I helped out a lot. There was such a wonderful view, it was bound to get redeveloped. The owner wanted us all out. He said it would become the playground of the Midlands.' (S. Tarpley)

Laura Sargent (standing, right), with girlfriends in 1918. Marriage and the right to vote were two big changes soon to happen in her young life. She went to work at the Brooke Ladies Dress Factory in Clarke Road (see p. 51) which has since been replaced by a block of flats. (G. White)

Gordon White and his dad in Harlestone Woods on the Althorpe Estate, c. 1933. Gordon said: 'It was a good place to go for a day out, take a flask and that. In the holidays if we went anywhere it was to visit family or friends. We had relations at Nether Heyford, 7 miles away. They took me for a fortnight. Roads weren't so busy so I biked. I went to Skegness for half a day, by train, before I was nineteen.' Jeremy Seabrook observed that: 'Children were born for the boot and shoe trade, casually employed and sacked for drinking or singing. There was no room for ambition. Children copied their parents and heeded adults. They laboured for treasures like a Windsor chair, a cord sofa, vase or gas stove.' (G. White)

Gordon White with the treasure his father won for him at Abington Park Fair in about 1933. He said: 'We shared a house with my grandparents. Grandad used to mend my boots. He looked at them and said, "You'd think these belonged to a one legged boy because, you bein' always on that scooter, only one of 'em's wore out!" Our house was in the shadow of Crockett & Jones' shoe factory and schooling was in Stimpson Avenue. I had the cane several times. The teacher was very calm and deliberate. You never had it unless it had to be used. But I was more harmed by what happened to me at the shoe factory than at school. Comics like *Wizard*, *Hotspur* and *Rover* gave me lots of pleasure. I got my first camera, a Kodak, on special offer.' (G. White)

Gordon White's mother, Laura Sargent, walking with a friend in Harlestone Woods in about 1950. Laura lived into her nineties and saw great changes to her home town. When she married, she and her new husband moved into the back rooms in her parents' house. Those were the days when the extended family made up for lack of money. (G. White)

Gordon White with his classmates in 1937, his last year of school. They had cycled out to the bridge at Blisworth with their teacher Mr Harris, whose nickname was 'Slasher' because he used to slash at the boys with his cane. I suppose he was only trying to keep them on the rails – just like the train driver in the next picture. Blisworth was a popular venue for picnickers who came to watch the West Coast expresses roaring past. In 1838 Stephenson's main line bypassed Northampton because the engines were not powerful enough to climb out of the Nene Valley. Local landowners did not want the railway anyway, although the *Northampton Mercury* reported in 1845: 'The town which has not a railway in its vicinity is an exception, isolated, shut out from the rest of the world.' (G. White)

This is what the boys were waiting for at Blisworth in 1937, a train so popular that Hornby models of it are collectors' items: the 'Coronation Scot', here streaking past a waiting goods train. Streamlining enabled speeds of up to 114 mph and broke the existing speed record on a test run in the same year. The London Midland & Scottish Railway Company (LMS) painted blue and silver stripes along the length of the train. (G. White)

Gordon White reflected that: 'At school we progressed from chalk and slate to pen and ruled exercise books. By then we were ready for the outside world.' And here they are taking a look at factory life far away at Ford's Dagenham car factory. What a treat just before going to work in factories themselves. Gordon said: 'The move from school to G.T. Hawkins' factory was absolutely traumatic. The factory was a dirty filthy place and safety regulations non-existent. I witnessed quite a few accidents. But all that was in the future when Mr Harris took us on this trip. We went by train to London and up the river by steamer to Dagenham. We had tea on the steamer coming back.' (G. White)

Express Lifts' annual carnival parade entering the Abbey Works, *c.* 1920. All big companies promoted social activities and summer relaxation. Northampton-born writer Jeremy Seabrook contrasts today's rich with those of the past, suggesting that now they have no sense of guilt or concern about those less well-to-do (*The Everlasting Feast*). (Express Lift Co.)

Express Lifts' Christmas Party, 1952. There was nothing like the magic of Christmas, and large firms rewarded employees' children with a feast and visit from Santa. (Express Lift Co.)

Express Lifts' sports day and fête, 1950. The old Abbey Works stand beside the playing field. This is playtime but it's back to work on Monday. Most factories had sports grounds and Gordon White remembers that the finals of his 1930s school sports days were held at the Tru Form factory ground. For football or cricket they had one period a week at Abington Park. (Express Lift Co.)

Express Lifts' bowls club, 1952. The green is immaculate, and the turn-out indicates a company mindful that 'all work and no play' does not produce the best workers. The white ball is the jack and the object is to get your balls as close to it as possible. One veteran player said: 'They asked me to get close to the "jack". I said, "I don't know about that, but I've been close to the 'Jill' many a time!".' (Express Lift Co.)

Express Lifts' sports day, 1951. Here's dad showing the kids the proper holiday spirit. Bowls used to be a game for senior citizens only until television 'discovered' it, adding the essential ingredients of glamour and money. (Express Lift Co.)

May Queen celebrations at Little Houghton, a few miles east of Northampton, in the early 1930s. Villages then were more self-contained. Folk visited Northampton to buy and sell goods at the market. (N. White)

'Anyone for tennis?' This is late 1950s-style relaxation at the Express Lift Company's tennis courts. The ladies are wearing long white dresses giving them an air of charm and mystery wholly lacking in the modern centre court Amazon. But then it was all just for fun and not for big money. But economics rules. That's why these courts became a visitors' car park during the 1980s and why the factory closure was announced in July 1996. Owners GEC sold out to American giant OTIS who saw the factory as a branch that needed pruning. (Express Lift Co.)

All sorts of childish naughtiness is forgiven by today's 'understanding' professionals and the parents they 'enlighten'. Will today's children grow up in a world truly of equals or are they being misled by just another load of dreamers and ideologists? This is 1950s-style dreaming. 'I'm forever blowing bubbles, pretty bubbles in the air, they fly so high, nearly reach the sky, then like my dreams they fade and die'; so the song went and, being rather pessimistic by nature, it was one of my favourite ditties. (Express Lift Co.)

Meanwhile the show goes on. The girl on the left proudly displays her Notre Dame school blazer in the company of some senior role models at the Express Lifts' fête in 1952. (Express Lift Co.)

A cheap night out at Express Lifts' social club in 1948. These men worked hard and played gently. Dominoes is the name of the game and they are taking it all rather seriously. I wonder what they were talking about – the changes in store perhaps, or maybe they were just enjoying the peace. It looks like Friday night and they would probably be off to the allotments next day. Jeremy Seabrook observed: 'There are old men who still cultivate an allotment which becomes more overgrown each year and the produce of which they can scarcely give away.' (*The Everlasting Feast*, p. 221.)

Are these the upper echelons at the Express Lifts' social club in about 1950? They are engaged in the more cerebral game of chess, but there is just as much smoke in the air. No one told them how dangerous it was. People rarely believe anything that the authorities have not told them, especially since the post-war mass media explosion and the demise of the extended family. (Express Lift Co.)

A beautiful baby competition at the Yardley Hastings Memorial Hall a few miles east of town, *c.* 1950. People are perhaps more competitive about their offspring these days: 'Baby talk weds all the women together in easy association, a need for comparison and competition that reassures them that their child's development is normal, or preferably slightly better than normal.' (*The Everlasting Feast*, p. 199.) (*Northampton Chronicle and Echo*)

Alderman J.V. Collier jnr presents the Northampton Machine Company's angling trophy to H. Goodger at the Whyte Memorial Hall in Fish Street, 27 May 1954. The occasion marked the election of NMC's managing director, J.V. Collier jnr, to Mayor of Northampton (*see* p. 100). Here he is wearing the chain of office and following in his father's footsteps. (Simon Collier)

Simon Collier with his partner at the NMC Christmas party at the Salon de Danse in 1957. It would not be many years before the full weight of company responsibility fell on his young shoulders, but in the meantime all he has to do is face the music and dance. Margaret Thatcher (née Roberts) used to visit her uncle John Roberts in Northampton, where he had a workshop making pianos and church organs. He let her play one and she said she was quite good. But her brief musical career ended when she stopped lessons to prepare for university. With a bit more encouragement from her Uncle John, world history might have been different, and she could have been a regular player at this historic venue, established by John Collier in Weedon Road and named first after Queen Victoria's favourite prime minister, Lord Melbourne. John Campbell Franklin bought the premises, including the Salon de Danse, in 1886 and named them after himself. He later sold out to a company which extended into the old Abbey gardens, adding a sports ground, bike track and bandstand. (Simon Collier)

Members of the Collier family with friends at the cricket club dinner in 1958. Northants has a fine cricketing tradition. Local star Colin Milburn was a Test legend from the 1960s while Frank 'Typhoon' Tyson took 7 wickets for 27 runs in a single Test in Australia in the 1954/5 season. (Simon Collier)

Every major company fielded a cricket team until the efficiency drives of the 1970s when world competition got even tougher. This is the Express Lifts' office and works team posing before a match on 31 May 1952. Terry Tarpley, who did his engineering apprenticeship at British Timken, said: 'Timken *was* Northampton at one time. There was great rivalry with Express Lifts if we played them at cricket.' Terry is in the next three pictures. (Express Lift Co.)

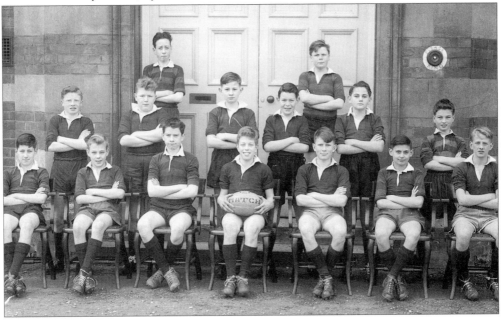

Good sportsmen have to start young. These are pupils at the prestigious Northamptonshire Grammar school, chosen for the rugby team in about 1958. Boys in those days were always addressed by their surnames, a tradition I will follow here. The two at the back are Robinson (left) and Brind. In the second row, left to right: Manning, Robinson, Jeffries, Tarpley, Barrit, Stapleton. Front row: Mason, Hull, O'Brien, Taylor, Gardiner, Soames. (T. Tarpley)

No good grammar school neglects cricket. This is Northampton's school team for 1960. Back row, left to right: G. Ashby, R. Cornelius. Second row: A. Mason, T. Tarpley, L. Harrison, T. Morgan. Front row: M. Parsons, G. Stacey, R. Smith, M. Henderson, J. Pettigrew. (T. Tarpley)

There are few more relaxing sights than a village cricket team at work. Here is Cogenhoe's team, down from the hills and posing in all their finery on the racecourse in 1968. The team includes Brian Foley, Les Robjohns, Geoff Waldren, Bob Sketchley, George Adkins, Brian Godsiff, Ted Mann, David Bliss, Alf Merritt. Horse racing ceased here following serious accidents, the Jockey Club pronouncing the course unfit for racing on 27 September 1904. But racing enthusiasts don't have far to go for an alternative venue – Towcester is only 8 miles away. (T. Tarpley)

Express Lift Co. staff prepared for an away game in about 1953. The luxury coach in the background assures them of the best comforts en route. Northampton's first motor bus services started in 1923 and soon rivalled the trams. Services were gradually extended beyond the tramway's limits, reaching outposts such as Far Cotton and Kingsthorpe. (Express Lift Co.)

Express Lift employees taking refreshments at the Fox and Hounds pub, Harlestone, in the summer of 1955. Car ownership was still only for the élite at this time. The staff had been competing in a company car rally, an increasingly popular relaxation on the then uncluttered country roads of the county. (Express Lift Co.)

Express Lifts' car rallies were open to the alternative motorist. This good old British motorbike combo's 'pilot' is checking his bearings. He's brought two navigators to give him the edge! What a collector's item that old AA badge on the front fork would make today. (Express Lift Co.)

Gordon White found his German NSU motorbike a great liberator after the war. 'I did a lot of touring with my mate,' he said. Sadly the British motorbike industry has been decimated by foreign competition. In the good old days Albert Beard of Burns Street motorized a bicycle and 'Cedos' became an outstanding local name in motorcycling. The Northampton Motorcycle Club was formed in 1905 and established the tradition of the Boxing Day scramble at Tunnel Farm, Blisworth. Cllr A. Catt, leather manufacturer and inventor of penny-slot machines, was a founder member of the club, who went on to establish an endurance record of 2,557 miles in six days on a Triumph. His son Albert jnr was the first to wear coloured racing leathers, to match his purple Scott tank, at the Isle of Man TT in 1923. (G. White)

How about these for 'Bovver boots' at Stricklands in Clare Street? Coco the Clown, from Bertram Mills circus, has just popped in for a fitting in April 1957. Coco looks quite fashionable in a baggy suit that many an eighties stockbroker would have been proud to be seen dead in! Doc Marten's famous boots were actually made by another local firm, Griggs. Originating in Germany before the war, they comprised a rubber sole with air pockets, rather like an egg box pattern. (*Northampton Chronicle and Echo*)

Errol Flynn with former Northampton Repertory colleague Freda Jackson (centre), wife of local artist Henry Bird, and Errol's third wife Patricia Whymore. Errol was the legendary ladies' man, who once offended a female reporter by showing her an artificial appendage made by a film props department to enhance his outrageous reputation. Errol said his Northampton days were his best – but I bet he said that to all the towns! Here he is about to leave Sywell aerodrome after visiting a fête in Franklin's Gardens in June 1954 to raise money for the Little Theatre building fund. (*Northampton Chronicle and Echo*)

With so many theatres and so much home-grown talent there have always been plenty of stars in town to dazzle the man in the street. Here are the Beverley Sisters, with twins Babs and Teddie on either side of elder sister Joy. Evacuated to Northampton during the war, the twins worked for the *Chronicle and Echo* while Joy was private secretary to a local businessman. In their spare time they performed in 'Blitzcoveries' entertaining troops in close harmony style. Here they are promoting a Russon touring car outside Newland Motors' garage in the Market Square. (*Northampton Chronicle and Echo*)

Few stars glittered more brightly than Shirley Ann Field, shown here turning on the Christmas lights in Gold Street in 1960. Chauffeured around town in a black Rolls-Royce, she visited the Gaumont cinema, Dr Barnado's Home in Dallington, and Church & Co.'s shoe factory. She so touched local hearts that she was made honorary president of Gold Street Traders' Association, which had provided the lights. With her on board perhaps they thought they wouldn't need to pay for any more Christmas lights! Cllr George Nutt (left) was among the five thousand people dazzled by the display. (*Northampton Chronicle and Echo*)

The Beatles, the biggest stars of all in the 1960s, were allegedly more popular than Jesus. Here they are visiting the ABC cinema on 6 November 1963. Their ten-song concert reached fever pitch with 'Twist and Shout'. Whatever their merits, the Beatles became a leading export and were honoured by the prime minister. On this occasion they had to be sneaked out via the back door and through a factory to St Michael's Street where a fast car was waiting to speed them to London. They didn't even wait for the National Anthem. (*Northampton Chronicle and Echo*)

The support act for the Beatles concert was Peter Jay and the Jay Walkers. Some of the girls got so excited they threw their underwear at their heroes. The ABC was one of the longest surviving cinemas from Northampton's cinema heyday, but it too closed in 1995. Harry Smith recalls the old Roxy near the station: 'It was a tin hut. We went once a week to the old silent films in the 1920s. We used to collect old buttons in a jam jar to earn money to go in. When we were older we got money from a paper round. We went to the Temperance Hall in Newlands where the Grosvenor Centre now is. We saw cowboy films on Saturday mornings. I remember seeing Al Johnson in "The Jazz Singer", the first talkie, at the Majestic. I was about six and went with my dad.' (*Northampton Chronicle and Echo*)

The giant cooling towers of Northampton power station provided a dramatic backdrop to all manner of fun and games in neighbouring Midsummer Meadow, but like much that comes and goes these days, they were judged redundant and blasted out of existence during the 1970s. Baden Powell worked for the Northampton Electric Light Company in 1936 when it was all new. At that time the field was called Cow Meadow: 'They used to have wooden poles before the pylons and the wires looked as harmless as clothes lines. The general foreman was smart and a proper old tyrant.' (Express Lift Co.)

A summer holiday in 1959 and these girls are making hay while the sun shines in Midsummer Meadow. Jean Wooding remembers swimming in the open air pool here, which was heated by chlorinated water from the power station. She said: 'You came out covered in little bits of black. The pool was filthy and the changing cubicles basic. But we liked going.' The meadow was used as a wartime services camp and the Cobblers football team trained on it. The pool was closed and demolished during developments in the 1980s. (*Northampton Chronicle and Echo*)

Abington Park putting green, February 1968. It was situated on one of the town's best parks. The original manor house here was known as Abington Abbey, though it was not a religious house. Built in the reign of Richard II, it was bought by Nicholas Lylling, whose only daughter Elizabeth married Robert Bernard. The Bernards lived here for 200 years until Sir John Bernard sold the manor to William Thursby for £13,750 in 1669. Thursby's family were in residence for the next 200 years, rebuilding the house on a lavish scale. Sadly they overreached themselves and had to sell the property to the Lloyds. Samuel Jones Lloyd became Lord Overstone in 1850 and his daughter married Captain Lindsay who became Lord Wantage. The house served as an exclusive asylum in Victorian times but in 1892 the Wantages gave it, together with twenty acres, to the town. The council bought another forty-two acres and opened the park in 1897. (Northampton Borough Council)

Looking south from Delapre Abbey, 1970. Built in 1145 and dissolved by Henry VIII in 1538, the Abbey and grounds eventually passed to the Bouverie family. When the last of these died in 1943, the property was bought by the council. The building was taken over by the Record Office in 1958 and the grounds became a public park. (Northampton Borough Council)

Now I know why they are sometimes called birds —
by more vulgar folk than I! This is Susan Seaward
leaping into the air at the Art Revel Ball, December
1961. Her figure-hugging finery is somewhat
unusual, but such displays were once commonplace
at this venue, the Salon de Danse. They even held
fashion shows at the stately old Guildhall, and a
'lovely legs' competition at the appropriately named
Fanciers' Working Men's Club in Wood Street.
Thank the Lord for sociologists who are working to
end such outrages! (*Northampton Chronicle and Echo*)

An old army breakdown truck pressed into service to transport this blonde beauty, wearing the skin of a
beast, as a publicity stunt for Chipperfields Circus, through the crowds outside Castle station in October
1962. The truck was part of a procession to the showground at Midsummer Meadow. (*Northampton
Chronicle and Echo*)

Pardon the cliché, but oh, happy days! This crowd has gathered at Beckets Park to watch the carnival parade in 1962. Local poet Dominic Allard is fifth from the left in the front row. Musing on the changes in the town, he wrote: 'I recalled the bleakness that followed when the demolition workers had finished. There were streets of rubble where houses used to be.' And in his poem 'Clearance Area' he mused:

> Who can say now
> That anything was here,
> other than open land,
> used only by stray dogs.

(*Northampton Chronicle and Echo*)

Bags and panama hats are piled high on the steps while schoolgirls pose before the main entrance of Notre Dame School in Abington Street, in a moment of post-exam euphoria and joy at leaving school in 1965. Suzanne Tarpley (née Rollestone) recalls: 'We weren't supposed to use this doorway. Some girls set fire to their panama hats but they only smouldered. They were threatened with expulsion.' (S. Tarpley)

Suzanne Rollestone pictured in the backyard of Marefair sub-post office and newsagent in 1961, wearing her first Notre Dame School uniform. She said: 'It was a serge dress with detachable primrose yellow collar and cuffs. It was expensive – mum bought it from Sandersons and you could only dry clean it. This was done during half-term. Thank goodness the school changed to normal skirts and blouses. The nuns were very nice but they wanted to shield us from sex. The boys from the Catholic grammar school used to come down once a week for religious instruction and the nuns kept us well apart. But we left messages for them inside our desk lids! The school site was very pleasant but it couldn't keep pace with the facilities needed in modern schools. They had to hire a double-decker bus to take us to Kingsthorpe for tennis. The school was funded by a French order for all the Catholic girls in the borough plus a few assisted places. The nuns were buried in the churchyard.' (S. Tarpley)

The girls of Notre Dame School wore split shifts and bloomers for PE. Suzanne Tarpley recalls: 'The kit was modelled on Ancient Greece.' Bridget Hickey, on the far right, has taken the image a stage further and adopted a classical pose! The other girls, from left to right, are Barbara Buckley, Geraldine McKenzie and Vicky Finnis, with Diana Urquhart seated in front. They are pictured in the school gardens at the end of the summer term in 1965. Suzanne said the gardens were peaceful and relaxing. But the school moved to Kettering Road and was renamed Thomas à Becket. A developer bought Notre Dame and the whole site was bulldozed one Sunday in 1979. People protested and said it should have been listed, but they were too late and the space was needed for shops and offices. Jeremy Seabrook, commenting on the changes in town, ventured: 'It isn't reasonable to expect that those in positions of power should have any understanding of the community they are going to destroy; but when they set about their destruction with slogans about progress and future generations in their mouths, it is precisely through such people that the compulsion of an insatiable and joyless consumerism works. They are the unconscious agents of the new tyranny that has replaced the old coercive forces of poverty and want.' (*The Everlasting Feast*, p. 237)

Suzanne Rollestone in the back yard of Marefair sub-post office and newsagents, *c.* 1963. She is holding her kitten Moses and longing for the countryside from which her family had recently moved. She said: 'I felt very shut in. We used to have a huge garden, then we had this yard with Hamp's furniture warehouse at the bottom – Hamp's was a family firm trading in Freeschool Street.' (S. Tarpley)

But at least Northampton is well endowed with parks and all sorts of animal lovers. This lady is walking her rabbit in St Giles' churchyard in about 1984. (Pip Brimson)

Spring Lane Primary School sports day, *c*. 1964. Proud parents Eric and Kathleen Rollestone are at the winning tape to applaud the efforts of their daughter Judith. Now a lawyer working in London, Judith has come a long way from these snug terraces which used to be part of a self-policing community. Jeremy Seabrook commented on the inrush of community workers during the early 1970s: 'Only now that the community has irreversibly broken down do the community workers appear.' (*The Everlasting Feast*, p. 196.) He feels that 'to mourn with the old, as I do, is a sterile experience'. He suggests that even the most radical community workers are involved in a kind of consumption, 'living off a cultural past'. (S. Tarpley)

Would you let your teenage daughter go to a place like this? This is the Embassy Jazz Club in 1962, when teenage rebellion was becoming very big business, so there wasn't much to stop this young lady going barefoot to breathe the smoky air and ready to dance the night away. The permissive society flourished in the sixties and one consequence was the building of a home for unmarried mothers off Harlestone Road. This was dubbed 'the dump' by one of its inmates who recalled: 'One girl had her father's baby. She spent a lot of time staring at herself in the mirror.' (*Northampton Chronicle and Echo*)

A wise woman once said 'life's a cliché' and one is bound to use them. As I recall, in olden days a glimpse of stocking was looked upon as something shocking, and perhaps it still is. Lord knows what went on in caverns like this one, 'Gayeways' in Abington Street. Gordon White remembers: 'I used to like doing the quick step at Franklin's Gardens. When I see them leaping about nowadays I think they're all deranged. (*Northampton Chronicle and Echo*)

'Mirror Mirror on the wall, who's the fairest of them all?' Margaret Drabble, pictured here at the Denise Pitt-Drafen Dancing Academy in 1959, knows it's her. In those days women's lib was in its infancy and job opportunities for ladies in astrophysics limited. So instead of studying heavenly bodies she took to the stage – she was a shooting star, joining the Bluebell Girls and being named International Showgirl of 1968. Northampton was no stranger to showgirls. Harry Smith remembers watching them in 'nude style' reviews at the Royal just after the war; even the young curvaceous Shirley Bassey appeared there. He said: 'It wasn't shocking. I'd seen it all by the time I left the navy.' (*Northampton Chronicle and Echo*)

Gordon White pictured during a visit to Standens Barn Lower School, Flaxwell Court, in 1992. He said: 'I enjoy visiting and talking about shoe-making. The children listen to me and then have a go at making some out of cardboard. They write nice letters thanking me afterwards.' Gordon was born to be a shoe-maker. He recalls: 'When I took my eleven plus, which I didn't pass, it was just an ordinary day. The teacher said "stand up" and marched us out to a different school and a teacher we hadn't seen before. The exam was written on typed handouts, something else we'd never seen, we'd always used blackboards. We felt lost, wondering what this new teacher was going to be like. I was uncertain about what would happen.' (*See* page 17.) The school in this picture is a world away from the old Stimpson Avenue days of open fires in the classroom, clanking heater pipes and forty-two in a class. (G. White)

Sylvia and Gordon White outside their home at 72 Barry Road, enjoying retirement after a lifetime of hard work. Gordon remembers moving here in 1935 when the road was almost on the edge of town, close to the smallholdings and allotments. Now it's full of cars, many visiting the teachers' centre. Gordon said: 'They dug all the street up recently to install cable TV.' (G. White)

The start of the balloon festival on the old racecourse in 1992. (G. White)

The lady feeding these pigeons in Abington Street during the winter of 1995 was alarmed at being caught in the act of encouraging wildlife into the town centre. But why shouldn't the birds feed? Urbanization is a continuing threat to wildlife and the Northants Wildlife Trust is doing its best to protect the diminishing countryside. (R. Cook)

Queen Elizabeth tours Church's shoe factory in St James after taking lunch at the Guildhall on Thursday 8 July 1965. Stewart Kennedy is leading the tour and the Queen is followed by the Lord Lieutenant of the County. She next paid a visit to Earl Spencer's family home at Althorp. Sir John Spencer bought Althorp from the Catesby family in 1508 and became the county's biggest sheep breeder. The resulting wealth provided his grandson, another John, with money to build a new house at Althorp in 1572. Of the many royal visitors to Althorp, Prince Charles became the most famous, enjoying romantic moments with Sarah and Diana Spencer and finally marrying the latter. Diana reckons her noisiness rather than her looks drew Charles's attention during their ill-fated meeting in November 1977. The rest is history, as they say. The Spencers have enjoyed a turbulent past, which includes a political rise in 1768 when the 1st Earl put up his own candidate for parliament and protested when he was beaten by 612 votes to 537. Spencer won the argument over rule-bending and tightened the family's grip on local politics. In those days only the wealthy could vote, and votes were bought. Spencer started his own boys' school, with a distinctive uniform, symbolic of his power in 1770. (Church & Co.)

A PLACE TO WORK

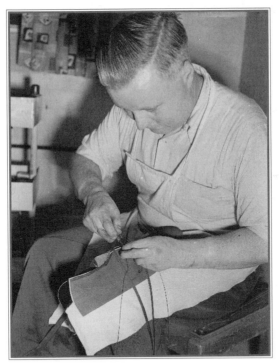

*Handmaking shoes at Mansfield Hospital workshop.
Gordon White was the last to work there, his starting
salary £12 10s for a 5½ day week in 1964. (G. White)*

Spencer Bridge, named after the powerful Spencer family, photographed on 2 October 1962 during reconstruction work. (Northampton Borough Council)

Northampton's first railway station was opened in 1845 at Cotton End and connected with the main west coast line at Blisworth, 4 miles away. This picture shows platelayers Albert Powell (left), R. Gutteridge (centre), and Boscoe Taylor, at Blisworth in about 1920. Albert's son Baden said: 'They reckon you could tell the time of day by the position of the peak on Boscoe's cap! Dad worked on the railway from 1900 to 1945. He smelt of the wood pickle which they used to preserve the sleepers, and creosote which they used on the wooden wedges [keys] used to hold the lines. They walked the line checking it ten hours a day. Then dad did his allotment when he came home. That was like an extra bit of money.' (Baden Powell)

Retired bargee George Beechey working at Cotton End Wharf, May 1964. He had seventeen locks to keep free from rubbish using a 20 ft long pole and a long rake which was called a keb. Remarkably he used to cycle from lock to lock carrying his tools. (*Northampton Chronicle and Echo*)

Looking towards Newland in December 1938, and all those bikes without security locks. Two belong to local traders. Gordon White recalls: 'Some boys left school to work as errand boys for high class provision merchants. They'd be perched on a high old bike with a tin plate advert for the shop attached to the crossbar, and they'd be wearing a long white apron. If they were all right, they'd progress to the provision department.' The hoardings give a clue to local relaxations, including an advert for Ginger Rogers at the Cinema De Luxe. Gordon White remembers before the war: 'We'd queue for the early door at one cinema and then dash out afterwards to catch another somewhere else.' (*Northampton Chronicle and Echo*)

Northampton Theatre Royal and Opera House, photographed on 10 July 1964, before redevelopment linked it with the Derngate Centre. The town's first recorded performers were Mr Jones's company of comedians from London, who opened on 21 June 1742. The Theatre Royal opened in Northampton's first gas-lit building, tiny premises on the corner of Marefair and Horseshoe Street, in 1824. John Franklin, hotelier and owner of Franklin's Gardens in St James, commissioned this building which was designed by leading theatre architect Charles John Phipps. It opened with *Twelfth Night* on 5 May 1884. Complete with stage and stalls located underground to keep it cool, the building cost £12,000 and could accommodate up to 1,500 people in its heyday. Refurbishment followed the fire of 1887 and improvements included plush upholstery, velvet hangings and a magnificently painted ceiling. From 1884 to 1926 it operated as a touring venue for opera companies including D'Oyly Carte's provincial premiere of *The Mikado*. (Northampton Borough Council)

Northampton shoe-makers photographed before their annual day out in about 1920. In the 1850s Henry Mayhew wrote: 'The boot and shoe-makers are certainly far from being an intellectual body of men. They appear to be a stern, uncompromising and reflective race. This is perhaps to be accounted for by the solitude of their employment' (*Morning Chronicle*). In 1869 Mr R. Rowe took a different view: 'A large proportion of the Northampton shoe-makers struck me as being of the alcoholic persuasion.' (G. White)

Shoe-makers, *c.* 1900. Gordon White describes them as 'the flat cap and muffler brigade'. He remembers someone asking why shoe-makers came out of the factory so fast when the whistle blew; he answered 'because we are used to doing everything fast. We have to.' Gordon's uncle Frank Sargent is on the left in the back row. Gordon said: 'We called our aprons pinafores. Some men never wore them, but I always did. Odd bits of leather which fell on the floor were called offal and we collected them in our aprons and it was sold to other trades. Anything big enough we used. Cleaning up the offal as a lad was horrible. I've had splinters halfway down under my fingernails from cleaning it off the floor.' (G. White)

Jim Sargent (back row, centre) left Northampton with these colleagues to try his hand at shoe-making in Canada during the 1930s. This was one way of avoiding the high unemployment afflicting the trade in that period, a time so hard that by the time the protestors on the Jarrow shipyard march, en route to Parliament, reached Northampton many had worn out the soles of their old boots. At least the war boosted demand for ships and boots, but most of these men died serving in the Princess Patricia's Light Infantry regiment during it. (G. White)

King Edward VII Memorial Hospital, 9 May 1964. There was no National Health Service until 1948 and the poor suffered from the lack of care. Many children were born crippled or became so and James Mansfield's donation of Western Favell as a hospital was an important beginning. Gordon White was the last man employed there – he left in January 1987 – making orthopaedic boots and shoes. Nowadays a multi-fit shoe is available and the job is redundant. The hospital amalgamated with Northampton General. Of the decaying building Ivy Bagle asked: 'Why has this building never been listed to help save it from the same fate as the New Theatre and Notre Dame School?' (Northampton Borough Council)

Northampton's prosperity relied on the efforts of men like these, working for the Northampton Machinery Co. (NMC) during the late 1930s. They were led by the great J.V. Collier snr, JP and Mayor of Northampton. His grandson Simon, who manages NMC today, said: 'My grandfather was one of the first to get a car after the first war. They made a one-way system around All Saints' Church (*see* page 8). He voted against it in council and for a long time ignored it. Those sort of men don't exist anymore, thank God. He was very autocratic but his strong personality was great for those times.' (Simon Collier)

The Brooke ladies' dress factory in Clarke Road during the 1930s, looking rather quaint and now long gone, replaced by a block of flats for the needy. Jeremy Seabrook described radical students graduating and coming to town for careers as 'trendy, gentle, pot-smoking seraphs in shabby Afghan coats soon bored and moving on.' (*The Everlasting Feast*, p. 226.) They occupied flats in poorer areas, 'perhaps with the idea of relieving Irish women of prams full of babies and washing, or of liberating belligerently contented women from the thraldom of the twilight shift at the local cosmetics factory'. (G. White)

Gordon White said: 'When I left the RAF in 1946 I wondered whether to go back to shoe-making. Then I found there was a full-time day course for ex-servicemen at Northampton College in hand-making shoes. There were a lot of ex-servicemen already demobbed and very limited choice between the shoe trade and agricultural engineering.' This picture shows the men on Gordon's course. The two men seated in front are instructor Fred Benching (left) and Stan Spittles. (G. White)

Sylvia White (left) at her retirement party at Fink's factory, 1990. She spent all her working life there making leather coats. She used to make fancy coats for the gentry. The 1960s were the beginning of the end of the old 'head down and keep at it ways', said her husband Gordon. (G. White)

A sturdy light van chassis posed on a Towcester estate, showing all it's got. They don't make them like this any more. (J. Ounsworth)

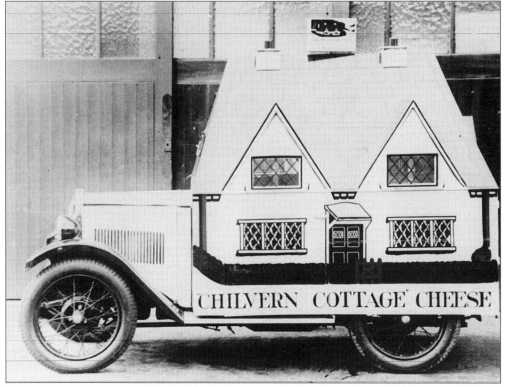

The chassis shown above would probably have received its body from the famous Mulliner coach-building firm in Bridge Street. They had made horse-carriage bodies since 1760 and adapted well to the motor age. Joseph Grose's Marefair Garage also diversified into vehicle body-building. His firm made some of the bodies for these Chilvern Cottage Cheese delivery vehicles. Northampton's first six-wheeler double-decker buses were also bodied locally. (R. Jellis)

Haulage contractor Gerald Butt at his desk in 1991. Behind him is a painting of company founder Charles Butt, a well-built man who joined the army under age and became one of their boxing champions. Gerald said: 'When I left school father said, "Go out and learn a trade, then please yourself." I finished my apprenticeship in 1958. After that came National Service. Then I went into our company workshops. You've always got to look to the future. Over the years Northampton has become one of the largest distribution centres in Britain because it's so central.' (C. Butt Ltd)

Quarrying has been an important local industry for years. This Priestman Wolf shovel has hitched a ride to the pit on the back of a C. Butt low-loader pulled by a Scammell Highwayman. It was photographed outside Wilson Plant Hire's Weedon Road depot in 1958. Company founder Charles Butt and his nephew were very much highwaymen themselves. Gerald, now 87, recalls: 'I left school to become a butcher's assistant. At seventeen I joined my uncle who'd just left the army and owned a horse and cart. We worked for the Corporation carrying road-mending materials and supplying the gangs looking after the tramway. We also carried household refuse to the incinerator in Castle Street and later West Street. We bought our first lorry in 1929 and got more business. We had about six vehicles when the government brought in licences and we were running daily to London.' (C. Butt Ltd)

C. Butt Ltd favoured ERF vehicles during the early post-war years, buying their first four-wheeler in 1948. This is their first ERF fitted with a Cummings diesel engine. Gerald Butt said: 'I served my apprenticeship with Blackwood Hodge in Northampton. They were UK agents for Cummings whose engines were fitted to the big Euclid dump trucks, used locally in the open-cast ironstone mining. Experience told me that those engines could take rough treatment and would be good in a road vehicle. We still run a few ERFs but Volvos are the backbone of our 200-strong fleet.' (C. Butt Ltd)

A long wheelbase AEC Marshall tipper from the C. Butt fleet loading gravel at Earls Barton pit during the late 1970s. In the early days hauling tanned leather from London and Liverpool was the main business. Hides were imported mainly from India. William Butt said: 'We carried on through the war. We'd start at 5 a.m. and hope to be back by 8 p.m. I remember when I got to Hockliffe I knew it was 29 miles and one hour to home. The roads then weren't too bad but the lighting was poor.' (C. Butt Ltd)

Iron and steel working used to flourish in the north of the county but the industry suffered rapid decline through EEC steel quotas, the recession and MacGregor's cutting hands. Here a redundant quarry engine is hoisted on to a C. Butt low-loader for delivery to the Peterborough Railway Preservation Trust in the 1970s. (C. Butt Ltd)

Heygate's spread Northampton's name far and wide. This articulated lorry is parked outside their flour mill in Tring. Heygate's is still a family firm, based at Bugbrooke Mill, in an area rich in good arable land, much changed since the days of water- and windmills. C. Butt also carried materials for local farmers. William Butt attributes his success to 'Bloody hard work. We had the will to do it. When lorries were delicensed I was one of the first to buy off government A licences. During the war most vehicles were commandeered for munitions. We benefited a lot from the decline of railways which used to carry all the leather. But nationalization of road haulage in 1947 was a setback.' (R. Jellis)

The Northampton Machinery Company's factory in Cleveland Road, which was opened by John Veasy Collier snr in February 1902 to make machinery for the increasingly mechanized boot and shoe industry. Encouraged by the demands of war, the company diversified into general engineering. Most of the factories built early in the twentieth century were driven by gas engines, many of which were installed and maintained by NMC. (Northampton Machinery Co.)

The Northampton Machinery Co. grew rapidly under the determined leadership of J.V. Collier snr. By 1914 a branch had been established in Leicester, another centre of British shoe-making, which was managed by Mr A. Irons. Mr A.G. Whitlock took over Cleveland Road's management for the duration of the war. In June 1915 the Ministry of Munitions ordered the firm to concentrate on munitions work. Valuable lessons in diversification were learned. This picture of the Balfour Road premises was taken just after the Second World War and presents a clean and tidy frontage for a company ready to face the challenge of a new age where communications would be the biggest business. (Northampton Machinery Co.)

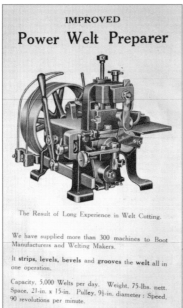

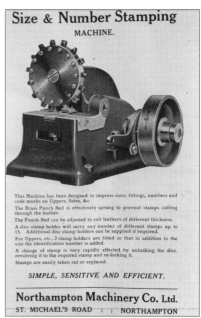

Two of the machines built for the shoe industry by the Northampton Machinery Co. The local shoe industry began with home workers. In 1818 there were some fifty adult male shoe-makers, most of whom were following their forefathers. This figure rose to three thousand by 1851, making shoes for Manchester and London workmen. They collected orders from their employers on Saturday and returned the next week to deliver the shoes and collect more orders. Mechanization and cheap foreign competition rapidly reversed the growth in these numbers after the Second World War. (Northampton Machinery Co.)

Inside the Northampton Machinery Company's Balfour Road Works, *c.* 1949. At this time the company made its own castings and the founder's grandson, Simon, took charge of this department when he had completed his apprenticeship. (Northampton Machinery Co.)

The Express Lift Company's Abbey Works, *c.* 1913. Crude lifts were used by Assyrians and ancient Egyptians. Treadmills provided power for their later models. Proper lifts, belt-driven and powered by factory steam engines, date from 1850. The Express Lift Co. was one of two twentieth-century companies specializing in making lifts. William Stevens founded the other one, which became Smith and Stevens, in 1770. They moved from London to Northampton in 1909 and as Smith, Major and Stevens built the Abbey works. Meanwhile Josiah Easton bought up French patents and prospered in the field of ship hoists and derricks during the First World War. GEC supplied the power units, backing Easton's Express Lift Co. The rivals pioneered electric lifts, before merging in 1930. GEC bought all the share capital in 1935. They made the company a landmark by building the 418 ft test tower which was opened by Queen Elizabeth II on 12 November 1982. (Express Lift Co.)

The Express Lift Company offices, early in the 1950s. Increasing automation and computerization of the workplace has forced a decline in traditional male skills and occupations. Even clerical work was once a male bastion, but women have come much more into their own since the 1950s. (Express Lift Co.)

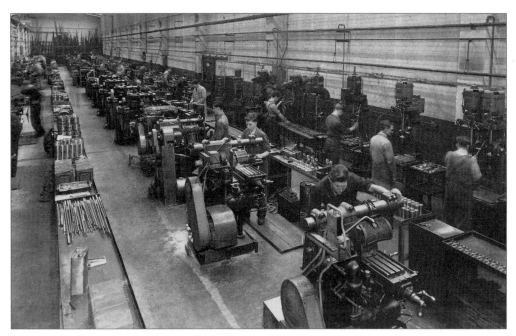

The Express Lift Company's Abbey Works at South Bay in April 1950. The company has been a world leader in supplying controlled lifts but shortly after GEC sold out to American giant OTIS, the new parent company announced closure in the summer of 1996. (Express Lift Co.)

The Express Lift Company's canteen, 1946. It's nice to have a sit-down and a bit of a chat after you've been busy all morning. This chap looks as if he's waiting to pay for his 'cuppa' – 'the cup that cheers but does not inebriate' – or maybe he's trying to pluck up the courage to ask one of those young tea ladies for a date. (Express Lift Co.)

The Express Lift Company's own firemen at the 1953 sports competition. Dave Wilson noted in his fifty-year history of the Mounts fire station: 'On many occasions, fires which would normally have to wait until the town brigade arrived, have been promptly tackled by firemen from the private fire brigades such as British Timken, Express Lift Co. or St Crispin's Hospital etc.' (Express Lift Co.)

This is the closing room at Church's St James factory, *c.* 1965. The environment is very clean and tidy. This company was at the forefront of health and safety consciousness. The workplace is dominated by women and the more laborious aspects of the trade have declined. (Church & Co.)

This man is nailing shanks at Church's St James factory in the late 1950s. 'Men used to hold the tacks in their teeth until the health hazard was realized. I started in the depressed 1930s. Our teacher looked out of the window of Stimpson Avenue School, toward Sears TruForm factory, and he said, "Those of you who don't pull your socks up will end up in there". I left school at 14 and ended up at Hawkins factory, starting on menial tasks – sweeping floors, fetching and carrying, watching and learning – then moved on to a simple job, going steadily further up the "ladder" till you got on to a machine. I couldn't wait to get into a man's job,' said Gordon White. (Church & Co.)

Church's East Street factory, c. 1975. This firm is one of the few surviving Northampton shoe-makers in a town which used to produce 10–12,000 pairs of military boots every week during the Napoleonic wars. Church's was founded in 1873 when shoe-making was progressing from hand craft to factory production, and their first base was in Duke Street. (Church & Co.)

Insole preparation at Church's St James factory, *c*. 1975. Machinery is necessary even for Church's high quality process. Managing Director Ian Kennedy said: 'The competition gets stronger all the time and comes from all parts of the world. But you can't buy shoes identical to ours from abroad. We use the best materials and superb lasts to create well-fitting shoes.' (Church & Co.)

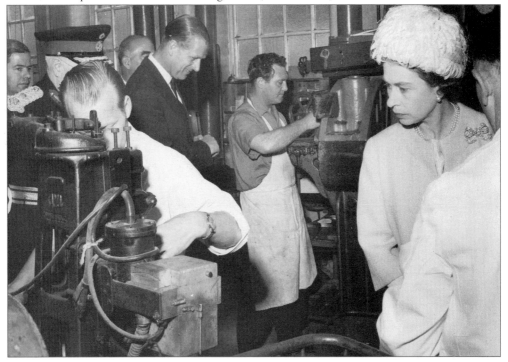

A royal visit to Church's St James factory. The Queen doesn't look too discomfited by the strong smells of glue and leather, nor the steady murmur of machinery. Prince Philip, in the background, looks as if he'd make a good factory inspector should anyone be foolish enough to abolish the monarchy. (Church & Co.)

Giving the shoes a good clean in the finishing department at Church's St James factory, late 1960s. Why are they one of the very few successful local shoe-makers? Joint Managing Director Ian Kennedy said: 'We are in a strong position, having concentrated on high grade products since the war. A solid base was built back in the days of Ian Church and Uncle Stuart Kennedy. Ian's father Lesley had a clear idea of how things were going and decided to protect our sales bases [see page 101]. We export worldwide, but 75 per cent of shoes bought in the UK are imported, mainly from the Far East where labour costs are one-fifteenth of ours. There are good factories in Thailand where skilled people are paid £36 per week for six eight-hour days, with few holidays and no social security. But our type of work is too specialized. They want volume. My job is a mixture of sorting day-to-day problems and trying to ensure that we're going to be all right in the next ten years. It's very difficult to take a long-term view when you're battling in the short term. We've got to see that our shoes have "Made in Northampton" stamped on them. But you've got to go where you can get the best deal. We buy most of our leather in France. We employ about 500 people in production, the same number as twenty years ago, but we're making more shoes. Our shoes are high quality process made and cost between £170 and £220 per pair. They're easy to repair. We are a solidly based company that has kept its roots in Northampton. There were about sixty companies before the war. Most have gone.' (Church & Co.)

Selecting lasts from Church's last room, *c.* 1975. Lasts are the wooden moulds over which the shoe's upper is shaped. (Church & Co.)

Albert Bennett making surgical boots at Mansfield Hospital in about 1962. Sidney Brown is in the background. Moses Phillip Mansfield set up his shoe factory in 1844 with his sons Harry and James joining as partners in 1878. James Mansfield was born in 1856. He became Council Leader in 1897 and was Liberal Mayor 1904–6. A religious non-conformist, he joined the Working Men's Club because he said he was one. He never attended trivial events but donated £1,000 to local poor, pledging two meals a day for local children during the severe weather. When the 1909 Old Age Pension Act was passed he invited all his fellow OAPs to tea. Tax problems drove him abroad in 1920 and he instructed Mansfield House to be sold in 1923. It didn't reach its reserve price so he donated it, with its grounds, to the town as a hospital for crippled children. (*Northampton Chronicle and Echo*)

Eric Rollestone outside his Marefair sub-post office and newsagents, *c.* 1967. The newspaper headline board blares out: 'Read it, blast you', which conveys nothing if not the arrogant and patronizing tendencies of tabloid newspapers which have increased in force over the years. Eric's daughter worked hard, helping her father in the shop and marking up newspapers for delivery. She remembers the old days: 'There was quite a community living over the shops in Marefair. I remember Greek Cypriots and all sorts. New property rates killed all that.' (S. Tarpley)

Church's glass and china shop in the Emporium Arcade which was in The Parade, Market Square, seen here in April 1968. Following redevelopment of the site, Church's relocated in the new Welsh House, but other businesses from the Arcade could not afford the new rents. Jeremy Seabrook noted that when the new consumerism came, 'The great mask of kinship began to unravel, the web of duties and obligations that had held people together in a tight structure of needs and responses started to fall apart.' (Northampton Borough Council)

Inside Toys R Us, St James Retail Park, March 1996. This is part of the new Northampton, where Jeremy Seabrook observed: 'Parents whose new role is made clear to them no less by clinics and paediatricians than by toy manufacturers and the baby industry, are equally certain that their new attitude is a revealed truth and they can only wonder that so many children survived the neglect and privations of the past.' (*The Everlasting Feast*, p. 150.) (R. Cook)

Carlsberg Brewery, photographed from Derngate in March 1994. The *Chronicle and Echo* described this building as a symbol of affluence in 1989. Brewing is a traditional industry. Phipps brewed in Bridge Street before selling out to Watneys in the 1960s and Northampton became home to the famous 'Red Barrel' which was phased out soon after. The more exotically named Carlsberg Brewery has taken over. There was much amusement from 1970s television adverts bearing an Orson Welles voiceover for the *Carlsberg Castle* sailing to Britain daily with its precious Viking brew when the true source was discovered. 'Carlsberg Castle' seems a more appropriate name for this building. The modern security camera in the foreground. This is actually watching the car park, a vital defence against increasing car crime and assaults in public places. One lady told Jeremy Seabrook in 1972: 'I don't even dare walk in the town after dark, the "characters" that are about now. Frightens you to death just to look at them!' (R. Cook)

Marefair in 1970 and the mud on the road tells us that developers are busy in the vicinity, but it looks as if they've sent a man with a shovel to clean up. A United Counties Bristol Lodekka bus makes a fine centrepiece to the scene. There were no fancy liveries for buses in those days, just a smart green. They used to operate from Derngate bus station which was replaced by a £10 million leisure centre during redevelopment in the 1970s. United Counties, formed as part of the 1920s National Bus Company, was sold off to Stagecoach during the 1980s Government deregulation of buses. (Northampton Borough Council)

A Ford Thames Trader lorry belonging to a local coal merchant parked in the Mayorhold, 30 April 1962. With so many locals moving into new centrally heated flats the coal man's business was beginning to decline. Dominic Allard recalls: 'My father was the last person in the town to use a horse and cart regularly for his scrap metal business. Whenever I stand near Bearward Street junction with the Mayorhold, I remember the days when I held the reins of the old horse while my father had a "half" in the Green Dragon public house. When ready, he would emerge to find the horse surrounded by a crowd of children fascinated by a horse and cart among the cars and lorries. The horse would receive a sharp instruction and off we would go down Horsefair and into Marefair, disregarding the traffic lights.' (Northampton Borough Council)

Clun Castle hauls an Ian Allan special train through Castle station early in the 1970s. The driver was Fred Bateman from Bletchley. Fred said: 'We worked hard. We were interested in our jobs and all mucked in. I had thirty-one years with LMS before nationalization. It took hours to get the locos fired up to make steam.' Railway work was hard and the drivers worked their way up to the élite jobs. But the trains couldn't run without rails. Gordon Pell's dad worked on the stretch between Northampton and Roade. He said: 'I used to take him up his meals when he was flagging. He used to have an old brazier going in the cold and put shots on the line to make small explosions when it was too foggy for signals.' (Robin Patrick)

Silverstone race track on the Northants border was converted from an old wartime bomber station. Grand Prix racing began there in 1948. The track is only a few miles from Lord Hesketh's stately home, Easton Neston, near Towcester. Hesketh ran his own Formula One team during the 1970s, promoting the talent of the eccentric James Hunt, World Champion in 1976. This shows the days of 'seat of your pants' driving, with Stirling Moss pit-stopping in the 1954 event. Notice the chap with the hefty microphone and deerstalker hat – is it a young Murray Walker?

Silverstone is only a few miles from the centre of town, which is handy for the local engineering company, Cosworth, of St James Mill Road, for many years a leading force in British motor sport. This picture shows the opening of their Costin House HQ on 22 September 1988. On the left is Keith Duckworth OBE, founder of Cosworth and honorary life president. Next to him is Mike Costin, co-founder and chairman 1988–90, and on the right is Jackie Stewart, former World Champion. Jackie will be leading a new team into the 1997 season financed by millions from his backers, the Ford Motor Co. (Cosworth Engineering)

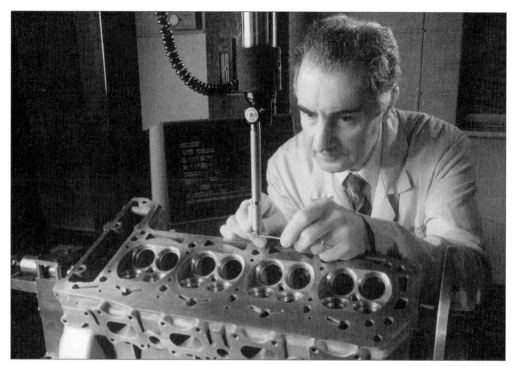

These days a good driver is lost without the best equipment. These are the experienced hands of Ted Dawson, long-term Cosworth employee, measuring a Mercedes cylinder head in the St James Mill Road workshops in about 1990. (Cosworth Engineering)

Twice Formula One World Champion Michael Schumacher at the Cosworth factory on 16 February 1994, posing behind the Cosworth Ford Formula One Zetech-R V8 engine which powered his Benetton B194 to his first World Championship. With him are the racing and Formula One design teams. (Cosworth Engineering)

TRYING TIMES

*Fire at the Wedgwood Restaurant, Abington Street, July
1984. Ironically it was a Berni Inn! (Pip Brimson)*

There was a First World War protest song called 'The Recruiting Sergeant' which included the lines:

As I was walking down the street,

I was feelin' fine and larky oh,

then the recruitin' sergeant said to me

well, you'd look fine in khaki oh.

But why should the simple men shown here on the square at Towcester, eight miles south of Northampton, appear so keen to follow the recruiting sergeant to war? Most of them weren't educated enough to understand the power politics of Europe's ruling élite who turned tiny Balkan states and chunks of Africa into pawns in a high class game. But few refused when the call came. Doubters were persuaded that if they didn't do their bit the dastardly Hun would overrun Britain, ravishing the women and killing babies. King George V and Queen Mary stayed at Althorp House in September 1913 and watched the largest-ever British troop manoeuvres – some 41,000 men took part. So the local men were charged with patriotism and ready to become 'Steelbacks' – the nickname for the local regiment, the Northamptonshire Yeomanry – when the call came. The Welsh Division arrived in 1914 and 16,000 men were billeted in Northampton. During the war 1,700 local servicemen died and hundreds were wounded, some of whom were brought back to Berrywood War Hospital. Many never properly recovered. Harry Smith recalls his father's slow death from the effects of phosgene gas: 'He was 30 when he died. He had been in the London Post Office Rifles and came to Northampton to be stationed on the racecourse before going to France.' Three civilians were also killed in 1917 when a Zeppelin dropped incendiaries. (Muriel Cousins)

Percy White, photographed during the First
World War. He was one of the first Londoners in
Northampton, having been born in the New Inn
yard near Liverpool Street station. He served in
the Royal Army Service Corps and his work
involved collecting cartloads of hay for forage.
This was delivered to the nearest railway stations.
He worked all around Brackley, Towcester and
Bicester, assisted by land girls. (G. White)

Jim Birch jnr joined the RAF as a boy entrant
during the 1920s, when horse transport was still
important, as his uniform reminds us. His father,
Jim snr, was a Northampton policeman. Uniforms
went with a secure type of job during the
depressed years between the wars. Jim snr was
transferred to South Wales where labour strife in
the mines created extra demand for police.
(G. White)

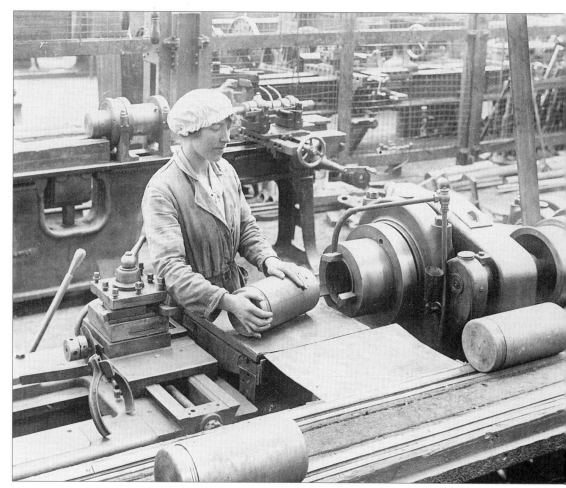

Making 'steak and kidney puddings' — otherwise known as shell cases for First World War artillery — at the Express Lift Co.'s Abbey Works in Weedon Road. At this time women already made up a fair proportion of the town's labour force, but war offered them the chance of greater responsibility and more skilled work. Factory safety legislation still had a long way to go, but this employer has taken the initiative by equipping his workers with hats to prevent their long hair from catching in machinery. Other factories, such as J.V. Collier's Northampton Machinery Company, were also engaged in war work (see p. 77). But large numbers of men were called away to war. On 4 August 1914 J.V. Collier and his father, Simon, a shoe manufacturer, were mobilized with their regiment, the Northamptonshire Yeomanry (whose Royal prefix was dropped as punishment for supporting Parliament during the English Civil War). They went to France the following November, where both served with distinction. J.V. was mentioned in despatches and Simon was awarded the Military Cross for gallantry in the field. He was killed on 14 September 1918. Many women were employed at Mr Collier's factory during the Second World War, and a number of them became skilled machine tool operators and inspectors. (Express Lift Co.)

Another view of shell cases being made, this time at the Northampton Machinery Co.'s Balfour Road factory. (Simon Collier)

John Veasy Collier snr, former Mayor of Northampton, had previously been manager of his father's firm, Simon Collier Ltd, boot and shoe makers. There he discovered a bent for engineering, inventing several machines for the factory. Beginning with a heel building machine, he advanced to a heel attacher which was approved for making army boots. Realizing the possibilities of mechanization in the boot and shoe industry, he left the shoe trade to start up his own engineering company. Acquiring a factory in Cleveland Road, he engaged a foreman, two men and a youth, installed some machine tools and began working on his own inventions. The firm suffered a severe loss with his death on 13 December 1937. (Simon Collier)

William Butt, 1992. He is still a guiding hand in the family firm he co-founded and which has prospered and moved into contract vehicle leasing. William said: 'When we were nationalized I became manager. But I bought two of my old vehicles from the new organization and ran them under a different name, within the allowed distance limits. That way I continued servicing local customers. You needed a special permit to go beyond a 25-mile radius from base and the railway companies always objected if you applied for one. Road haulage won in the end because it reduces handling times.' Looking back on changes to his home town, William said: 'As a lad I can remember Saturday mornings seeing cattle driven through the main road of St James, to and from market. Drovers were a regular sight on a Saturday morning, with cattle coming mostly from Ireland via Liverpool to Far Cotton station. Those that weren't sold were driven to Hill Morton, Rugby, on foot. They were a smashing sight, about fifty of them taking it easy. Those drovers were a rare old breed. Today everybody is in such a hurry to get everywhere. There's no doubt people used to be a lot more friendly. You knew each other more. But life was hard. I only needed medical attention once. In 1917 I was taking my father's horse up to his market garden at Dalington and there was another boy on the back with me. He slipped and pulled me off with him. I hurt my arm. Dr Milligan said I had badly sprained my elbow and strapped it up at a right angle. But it turned out it was badly broken and I haven't been able to move it since.' (C. Butt Ltd)

Roy Gardner and Gordon White in Air Training Corps (ATC) uniform. Gordon said: 'When the war started, because my education was limited, I had little chance of becoming aircrew. I was always interested in planes and followed the adventures of Amy Johnson, Scott and Black. I wanted to be a flier. With a pal I joined the ATC (then the Air Defence Corps). We used an old factory in Portland Street and were kitted out in RAF uniforms. We had lectures every evening and general parades on Thursday nights. They paid for evening classes on subjects like maths at Northampton College in George's Avenue. I volunteered for aircrew in 1942 and went to Cardington for attestation on maths and physical fitness. We all wanted to be pilots, but I settled for wireless operator/gunner. (G. White)

Northampton ATC photographed in the Exchange cinema foyer during the screening of 'A Yank in the RAF', starring Tyrone Power, in 1942. The girl on the sail-plane is an usherette and the cinema manager is just visible on the right, with Peter Rideout standing next to him. When Rideout was demobbed from the Navy in Australia, he joined the Australian Air Force and settled there (P. Rideout/G. White)

Looking rather like Charlie Chaplin in 'The Great Dictator', this is Stanley Seamark outside Derngate bus station, offering not-so-light reading to travellers. Did this peace-loving chap have a reasonable point of view? What would have happened if he had won the argument? Would Hitler have conquered Europe? Cynics might say that Germany did that anyway. There was the 'ethnic cleansing' – how could that be ignored? Again, Europe has experienced even that recently. At least, except for a Stirling bomber that crashed in George Row, Northampton had a fairly quiet war. American servicemen brought the first taste of foreign tourists. For them the area had special significance because George Washington's family originated from nearby Sulgrave Manor. (*Northampton Chronicle and Echo*)

The boots are now on Gordon White's feet instead of being crafted by his skilled hands. Here he is, ready for action. He said: 'My father was teetotal and mother only drank at parties. But I drank regularly when I got overseas. They served up local brews in the RAF mess. We found shorts as cheap, if not cheaper. When I came home I'd been used to drinking and went out with my pals to pubs in the town centre, like the Lord Palmerston. That's a burger bar now. Many of the old pubs have completely gone. We had our gratuities in hand and couldn't wait to hand them over to the brewers.' Jean Wooding said: 'Men must have found it difficult coming back from the war and finding women doing their jobs, and some of them doing it better.' (G. White)

J.V. Collier jnr leading the Duke of Gloucester on a factory tour at the Northampton Machinery Company's Balfour Road Works during the Second World War. During the war the firm was mainly engaged on making small arms ammunition machinery, machine tools and special tools for making submarine detection equipment. (Simon Collier)

The Northampton Machinery Company workshop, photographed in the early 1950s, during the transition period from the old boot and shoe making equipment to cable-winding machine making. (Simon Collier)

Evacuees from London disembarking at Northampton Castle station, August 1941. The faces suggest that some of them are enjoying their adventure. Some found better living conditions in their new billets than they had at home in the London slums. One story related that one boy from a large East End family arrived at a well-to-do home with his mother. After taking refreshments in the sitting room, the young urchin stood up and urinated on to the Axminster. 'Surely your boy knows better than that,' screamed the lady of the house. 'Course he does, go and do it in the corner,' screeched the scraggy mother. (Northampton Record Office)

Women moved easily into traditional male occupations during the war, encouraged by their achievements in the earlier conflict. The new war offered even more opportunity for them to prove themselves as men were once again forced into uniform to fight for a better world – but with no guarantee of houses or jobs when they returned home. This young lady is set to take over a job on the buses and she looks keen to show that she's not just a pretty face by getting to grips with what's under the bonnet. (Northampton Chronicle and Echo)

Local factories were converted to war work, and the surrounding countryside was dug, planted and harvested for victory. An army of land girls descended on the area. Women were drafted into all sorts of occupations under the Essential Work Order and who better to jolly them all along than the great man himself, Winston Churchill? In this picture it is all over and he is on the election circuit at Daventry. He expected his Tory party to be re-elected in gratitude and respect for his wartime leadership, but was disappointed. Much was expected of the new fangled socialism, which had not been given much chance to succeed following the 1929 Wall Street crash. The brutal war had created fresh hopes and idealism. (*Northampton Chronicle and Echo*)

Among those fresh hopes was the old chestnut 'Homes fit for Heroes.' But this was a tall order in a country virtually bankrupted by the war and the loss of its rich empire. Britain was hardly back on its feet by 1969 when these prefabs in Drayton, Kingsthorpe, were about to be demolished. A vast council house building programme was instituted throughout the 1960s but this was a burden on the rates, each unit costing the council far more than it was permitted to recoup in rent. This led to the Thatcher Government's 'right to buy policy' for tenants which in turn compounded the housing shortage for young or low paid. The more the town boomed, the worse the problem became. (Northampton Borough Council)

Upper Mounts fire station, early 1960s. Mr A.L. Dixon performed the opening ceremony in 1935. The station was built on the site of the old prison to cope with the needs of the expanding town. When young firefighter Dave Wilson first set foot inside he said: 'I felt like Tom Thumb, the machines were so big. I never thought of being a fireman until I got laid off as a roofer working at Stoke Bruen museum in the winter of 1963 and I knew someone in the brigade. I had two weeks at The Mounts then went off to training school. It frightened me, but looking back from over thirty years later I know I'd do it all again. There were highs and lows but I never had that Monday morning feeling. Sometimes in the middle of the night with the blue light whizzing around I'd wonder what the hell I was doing at whatever incident I was at. Firefighters become very macho. Maybe it's a defence they put up. I've been caught in a wall collapse, trapped in a building, down holes, on motorways with cars piling up and not enough manpower to get people out. But when your back's against the wall you cope. You switch off. I've seen car suicides and dead kids when the motorway first opened. Your prime duty is to save life. The strike in 1978 was a terrible time but I supported it. Governments year in and year out kept putting us down, but 99 per cent of us kept our kit in our car boots and would have responded if there had been a major incident. It was a terrible time, causing a lot of animosity, lost homes and broken marriages. Modern fast-track promotion produces different sorts of people, but you need some who are good administrators. Women have problems if they're just out to prove a point. If they're just trying to do the job they're OK. Problems can arise on the physical side because ladders can weigh two or three cwt and even some men can struggle with them, but when there's three people to a ladder you have to pull your weight. Anyway the equipment will change, it will get lighter.' (Northampton Borough Council)

The west side of The Drapery, April 1968. This unusual shot emphasizes the bicycle casually parked in the foreground. I wonder when they suddenly became worth stealing? Judging by the amount of rubbish stacked up in the street those dustmen must be on strike again. Still it's not as bad as the mayhem around this area back in 1926 when Mr Cameron, the Tramways manager, thought he'd help beat the General Strike by driving a tramcar up to the junction with Mercer's Row. There a crowd of strikers tried to remove all the passengers. Police made a baton charge, arresting the ringleaders. Jean Wooding left school in 1949. She said: 'You can talk to anyone my age and they'll say it's not as nice in town now. Down Abington Street you met all people that you knew. There were the Kingsthorpe lot, the Far Cotton lot or whatever. But now it's turned into a big market town and has lost that little something. Now you go to big supermarkets and department stores. The shops that used to be down The Drapery in the fifties have all disappeared.' Philadelphus Jeyes was the most curious of these. Dr W.E. Brocklehurst remembers working there as a boy. 'It was established in about 1810. There were vaults under the road where orange wine was stored to settle and mature before being used to make "quinine and orange wine tonic". We produced everything from sterile injections to conditioning powders for horses and ointment for footrot in sheep. I was apprenticed there from 1935 to 1938.' His skills saved lives when he was a wartime prisoner of the Japanese as he was able to make medicines for his sick comrades. (Northampton Borough Council)

Northants Candy Queen, 1965. Teenager Suzanne Rollestone doesn't look too pleased with the situation here, even though she came second in the contest. She explained: 'Sharpes needed entrants and the rep persuaded my father (he kept Marefair sub-post office) to let me enter. I got a new black dress and the family all dressed up. We got to the door of the Salon de Danse and they said: 'You can't come in with a child' (Suzanne's sister Judith). I had a sixth-form friend with me, so my parents went off and had a meal, leaving me to it. I was petrified sitting with the rep and his wife, and walking up and down the Salon. There were only five or six entrants and the one who came third was old enough to be my mother. Everyone who took part had to be connected with the confectionery trade. The winner worked in a sweet shop. Everyone danced for about two hours afterwards.' (S. Tarpley)

The last embers of the fire at the Wedgwood Restaurant in Abington Street in July 1984 have been doused and the firemen can relax. Policeman David Brown and bus driver Bryan Spence saved two men trapped in the restaurant blaze. They climbed on to the roof of a double-decker bus to pull manager Nino Bartella and chef Derek Smart clear. Rubbish piled outside the building the night before appeared to have been the cause. (Pip Brimson)

Fire appliances attending a fire on the sixth floor of Beaumont Court flats, 12 April 1984. Life is much safer now than when the Great Fire of 20 September 1675 took everyone by surprise. That all started from an accident with a few hot coals, which caused a blaze that leapt easily across narrow alleyways, feeding greedily on a diet of thatched timber buildings. Modern construction is still far from fire-proof and the 1960s planners' penchant for high-rise buildings presented firefighters with new challenges. In the early days of organized fire brigades, insurance companies issued fire marks and equipped brigades who were allowed to deal only with insured properties. Northampton formed its first volunteer brigade in 1864 under the direction of Richard Phipps but until 1885 there was no fixed place for the fire engine and escape to be stored. Then the council chose a spot behind the Town Hall. The following year they rejected a request for electric warning bells in each fireman's home. In January 1894 the superintendent reported that fires in the borough had cost £11,847 over the year. The brigade was taken over by the police in May 1888 and in 1891 their equipment totalled 2 steamers, 2 manual engines, 19 long ladders, 40 lengths of canvas hose and 17 lengths of leather hose. The first motorized engine was a Merryweather, bought in 1910. It could reach 35 mph fully loaded. Major disasters and a wartime decision to form the National Fire Brigade accelerated developments in the fire service. By 1940 Northampton had its first fully enclosed fire engine, which meant the firemen no longer had to cling to the side of a speeding engine. (D. Wilson)

Nurse Jean Powell's retirement from Northampton General Hospital, mid-1980s. Jean looks perplexed as she receives a gift of alcoholic beverage from colleagues who believed she was teetotal. One might say it was a case of surgical spirit! The bottles were actually full of water. (Pip Brimson)

Briar Hill Estate, February 1996. Is this a dream or a nightmare? While I was here a local urged me to photograph children stoning a passing train. Jeremy Seabrook observed of Northampton parents: 'The truth is they live by expediency. They sense that they have become a dwindling force in the socialization of their children and that other agencies beyond their reach have taken over. . . . Their ideas of discipline and propriety have been supplanted by others that have somehow ousted them by stealth.' (*The Everlasting Feast*, p. 154). Meanwhile the kids can do as they please and there'll be all sorts of experts to excuse them until they are no longer kids. As Seabrook says: 'There is a kind of hereditary forbearance to which extreme youth is title.'

Nowadays external forces even tell royalty what to do — most notably the tabloid newspapers who have condemned with relish Prince Charles's apparent abandonment of his sweet Northamptonshire princess, Diana Spencer. How sour the once promising fruit of love has turned. In 1989, the Charter year, the local paper reported Diana as a popular visitor. She became the first Royal Honorary Freeman of Northampton. But the magic has gone. On this grey February day in Abington Street in 1996, the *Chronicle and Echo*'s billboard announces: 'Charles and Diana, Bishop Speaks'. The subject was divorce but passers-by did not seem to see the message. (R. Cook)

A borough car park attendant, near Derngate. Spring sunshine glints off the metal monsters behind him in early March 1996. Just before taking this picture I had been given a 'free' ticket by two young ladies who were leaving and I was reflecting on the fact that there are still some kind people in the world when this uniformed gentleman approached and informed me that the ticket was not transferable and I would have to buy my own. I ventured that some people might get very cross to hear him say such things. He agreed, adding that some people were reduced to tears if given a parking ticket. I asked if his job was stressful. He said it was less so than his previous career, selling insurance. Having left London over twenty years ago to start a new life in the Shires, he thinks it has been worth it but that generally people seem more stressed nowadays. (R. Cook)

Abington Street on a cold February morning in 1996. The message on the shop window says 'Everything Reduced.' Is the value of life reduced too? Unemployment and homelessness are widespread. It's amazing that in the same year that so much fuss was made about the fate of frozen foetuses, people can still find excuses for why so many people face a struggle even to survive. Poverty isn't new, but the experience is different from when whole communities faced it together, a time when, as Jeremy Seabrook observed: 'You were born, you were married, you worked, you had children and you died. Nobody dared affirm anything else.' (*The Everlasting Feast*, p. 160.) Then came the consumer society and devil take the hindmost. (R. Cook)

Poet T.S. Eliot said that war did not cure the disease but left it raging. Of course, it's nice to think he was wrong and that this sombre wreath-laying ceremony at the cenotaph during Regiment Week, July 1950, was helping to discourage war. But war disguises itself, finds new combatants and never goes far away. The violence of formal war has the virtue of uniting people against a common enemy, while the violence of peace divides communities, usually along class, ethnic and, increasingly, gender lines. (*Northampton Chronicle and Echo*)

WHO PAYS THE PIPER?

*A lone piper playing a lament by the Market Square
entrance to the Grosvenor Centre, which opened in July
1975. (R. Cook)*

Delapre Abbey, built by the 2nd Earl of Northampton, Simon de Senlis, in 1145 on the site of a Cluniac Convent, was home to twenty nuns during the thirteenth and fourteenth centuries. Edward I stopped here en route from Harby in 1290, with the body of his beloved wife Eleanor – proving that some arranged royal marriages do work! He ordered crosses to be built at all five stopping places en route to Westminster, and this one was designed by John de la Bataille; it is still a landmark at the top of London Road. It stands on the edge of the former Abbey grounds, which are now Delapre Park. (Judy Ounsworth)

The Royal Standard flying over Church's factory during the Royal visit in July 1965. Crowns have been won and lost on Northamptonshire's battlefields. Mary Queen of Scots even lost her head in the county, at Fotheringay Castle in 1587. The Domesday Book listed William the Conqueror as the principal landowner in the county when most of it was forest and villages huddled in clearings. Barons looked after great estates, owing their allegiance to monarchs, but they weren't always trustworthy. Holdenby House, about ten miles north-east of Northampton, was once the largest private house in England and was bought by James I in 1607 as a hunting base. It also served as a prison for Charles I for four months in 1647 after the Scots had handed him over to Parliament. (Church & Co. Plc)

Abington Street, *c.* 1897. Sadly the buildings on the right, which housed the Notre Dame School, were demolished in 1979. How wide the boulevard is – it could almost be Paris! A horse-tram jogs along the centre carriageway; this was one of the early tram routes. The corporation bought up the Northampton Street Tramways Company for £38,700 in 1902. Horse-trams did not always travel gently. On one Saturday in 1902, car number 15, fully loaded, galloped out of control down a crowded Abington Street before overturning on the Wood Hill corner, killing one person and injuring twenty-one. (J. Ounsworth)

Looking north from The Drapery, *c.* 1895. Those were the days of acute class distinction. Frederick Hollis sold hats here, distinguishing upper- from middle-class customers according to whether they bought silk, tall or top hats. The tram lines indicate the presence of horse-tram services. The corporation did not start electrifying the system until 1904 and the first electric car ran on 21 July. The horses, which had been stabled in The Riding, were steadily replaced over the next ten years, the programme being completed on 23 October 1914. (J. Ounsworth)

A slightly earlier view of The Drapery displaying all the hustle and bustle of a busy market town. The area was originally known as The Glovery and has a long association with the cloth industry. Gwen Blane remembers going to Miss Chamberlain in The Drapery in the early 1960s to order her wedding dress. Her brother Dr W.E. Brocklehurst was apprenticed at Philadelphus Jeyes Drapery branch pharmacy. This was an important business, where the drugs were actually made and the young boy learned to make them. He would have preferred to be a doctor but his father, who was employed at the Railway Works, couldn't afford to send him to medical school. In those days medicine was a profession for the wealthy. (J. Ounsworth)

The Drapery, the view looking north, in 1969. The motor car has already made an impact. Trams disappeared from here in 1923 when no one considered the polluting effect of buses and cars. The emphasis was on transport flexibility and by 1935 buses were running from the town centre to Far Cotton, St James, Kingsthorpe, Western Favell, Lindsay Avenue and Mansfield Hospital, as well as on routes linking Kingsthorpe and St James. (Northampton Borough Council)

An aerial view of the Notre Dame School in Abington Street and the streetscape behind in the late 1950s. The school was demolished in 1979 and the site redeveloped. (S. Tarpley)

It's Monday morning, 31 January 1966, and these schoolkids have gone off to the ABC Cinema. No, the teachers weren't going soft before their time! The theme was the serious business of road safety and it was just as well. The town was soon to see a lot more roads and cars. Cinemas were always an exciting place for kids, but adults were the best market. Gordon Pell recalled two local cinema magnates: 'They were the Cipin brothers, hefty fat blokes. They owned the Ritz, Tivoli and Plaza. The Plaza later became a bingo hall.' (*Northampton Chronicle and Echo*)

This picture reminds me of J.V. Collier, JP and Mayor, who refused to obey the All Saints' one-way system. Today's traffic would make such rebellion impossible. Even so, motoring practices leave a lot to be desired, and though often comic they can be lethal. That's why comedians Laurel and Hardy were called away from their performance at the New Theatre to promote 'Car Safety Week' (19 to 24 October) 1953 in Abington Street. (*Northampton Chronicle and Echo*)

The masses had little option but to take the bus when this picture was taken in town in about 1920. Public transport started in 1881 with trams running from West Bridge to the racecourse. Gordon White recalls: 'When I first started work in 1937 there were few traffic signals. They had a constable on point duty for two hours while we thronged through the streets in the early morning. Then he cleared off and let the traffic find its own way. People would be getting off buses, riding their bikes. Folk used to charge you to park your bike in their side entries.' (*Northampton Chronicle and Echo*)

Waterways are the most gentle means of long distance inland travel and in 1763 Lord Halifax and Lord Northampton gave money to schemes to make the River Nene navigable in order to import cheap fuel. The next step was a connecting branch of the Grand Junction Canal via a 3,076 yd tunnel from Blisworth. Taking twenty-five years to build, it opened in 1815 and the *Northampton Mercury* reported: 'On Monday last was opened the branch canal between the River Nene at this town and the Grand Junction, which gives a water connection to all parts of the kingdom. The day being comfortably fine, a great multitude of persons assembled to witness the first arrival of boats, several of which were laden with various kinds of merchandise, and upward of twenty laden with coals.' This picture shows Cotton End Wharf, in March 1964. The bargee looks as if he's got that Monday morning feeling. His problem was heavy rain which had raised the water level in the Nene by about a foot over normal. This was too high for fourteen boats carrying grain and they were stranded for over a week. (*Northampton Chronicle and Echo*)

St John's Street station in the 1950s, all boarded up long before Dr Beeching's axe fell. It closed on 3 July 1939, and Bedford and Wellingborough passengers had to use Castle or Bridge Street stations. Several cars adorn the forecourt and would be worth a fortune on today's nostalgia market, where people hanker for the less hurried 'road rage'-free age of motoring. Bridge Street too had to make way for developers. (Northampton Borough Council)

Railway arches near St John Street station on the Wellingborough line being demolished, January 1973. A whole world of bonded warehouses and Victorian terraces, customs and curiosities went under the sweeping hammer blows of the dragline, the tracked vehicle in the centre. (Northampton Borough Council)

A traffic jam outside the British Railways (BR) goods exit by the Peter's Way traffic lights, 3 May 1962. BR's trusty Scammel Scarab (right) is waiting trying to get back in to drop off an empty and collect another full trailer. These vehicles were designed for rapid uncoupling and tight turning – they had a 15 ft turning circle as opposed to the 23 ft circle needed by a horse and cart. They were part of a plan for an integrated road and rail transport system. But the luscious lines of such cars as shown in this picture were too much for the travelling public and road transport became ever more popular. The Renault Dauphine (centre) was late fifties state-of-the-art, and its television ads sang: 'Whatever the load, she holds the road, the Renault Dauphine, a built-in heater, couldn't be neater, the Renault Dauphine.' Conversion to the motor age has almost been a matter of hypnosis! (Northampton Borough Council)

'You've never had it so good,' exhorted Tory Prime Minister Harold Macmillan as he faced up to the General Election of 1959. The electorate was already used to advertising slogans so he could easily avoid spelling out the details of his plans. This superficiality would backfire a few years later when the electorate reacted just as mindlessly to the media hysteria over the John Profumo sex scandal, which swept Harold Wilson into power. But for the time being Macmillan was on safe ground – except in Northampton where Tory Jill Knight played second fiddle to Labour sledgehammer R.T. Paget at this meeting in the Market Square. Paget's supporters got their own back for the jeering and booing meted out by the Tories during his 42-minute oration, by drowning out Jill Knight's 24-minute speech in the same way. Paget was returned with a majority of 2,700 votes in a record 83 per cent turn-out. He served as Northampton MP until 1974, witnessing the early effects of the 1960s South-East Economic Planning Council's (SEEPC) scheme for the region before going to the Lords. In 1975 the SEEPC planned four major swathes of development stretching away from London and making full use of existing and planned motorways and mainline railways. The planning group hoped to concentrate growth in these areas while keeping the surrounding countryside under strict planning controls (but Nicholas Ridley changed all that in 1988). Northampton was caught up in one of these swathes. County planners were also concerned about the effects of Milton Keynes new town, then growing fast toward its borders. Land prices inevitably rose and attracted a flurry of speculative development in the south Northamptonshire green belt. Labour's President of the Board of Trade addressed the town in August 1966: 'Northampton is already one of the main industrial towns of the Midlands. The big expansion now planned will bring problems, but I am sure Northampton will meet these with confidence.' (*Northampton Chronicle and Echo*, 15 August 1966)

J.V. Collier jnr, Mayor of Northampton, photographed at a celebratory reception and dinner at the Whyte Melville Hall in Fish Street on 27 May 1954. The main meal consisted of cold ham and tongue, and they toasted 'the Queen'. The new mayor described his first private engagement as a wonderful climax to the day and was given a great ovation by 200 employees. He went on to say: 'I talked in the council chamber of the family firm. Can I ask you not to think this means a lot of tripe? It is worth a lot these days when the whole structure of life is getting less personal.' Mr Collier was a leading member of the local Conservative Party. J.V. Collier's son Simon said: 'There was terrific potential for change in the 1960s, and they had a great town to start with. They could have made a feature of the river between St Andrews and Bedford Road, for instance. Some lovely old buildings disappeared, like the Peacock Hotel. There wasn't enough thought, it all happened too quickly.' Mr Collier's family firm now concentrates on making cable-winding equipment. Simon Collier said: 'There are just a few big players in the industry. We succeed because of quality of service and willingness to go out worldwide and sell.' (S. Collier)

Senior managers at one of the Church Shoe Company's retail outlets, *c.* 1965. From left to right, they are John Ashley, Jack Johnston, Stewart Kennedy and John Church. Joint Managing Director Ian Kennedy said: 'Our retail HQ is in Eastbourne. There are 100 shops in Britain, 30 (and a small factory) in Canada, 9 in France, 2 in Belgium and 1 in Italy. We export 70 per cent of our shoes worldwide and are in a strong position. Our management saw retail polarizing into the British Shoe Corporation and Timpsons. The retail base was shrinking fast, therefore we had to start our own.' (Church & Co. Plc)

John Church (left), joint Managing Director of Church & Co., outside Heathfield Way factory on 12 December 1994. He is escorting some Japanese visitors, which speaks volumes for the prestige of the company worldwide. (Church & Co. Plc)

Church & Co.'s old Duke Street factory shortly after electric motors were installed early this century. This was an important step forward in safety and efficiency for a company which has always been ahead of the field. Gordon White recalls another world in Hawkins shoe factory: 'If there was an accident in that bedlam of noise and the off switch was in the distance, it could be some time before action was taken. There were belts up to 40 ft long and they could break or come off pulleys. I once saw one snaking about until it hit someone on the head.' (Church & Co. Plc)

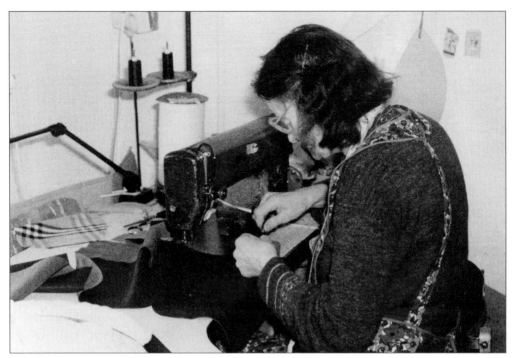

Nose to the grindstone at Finks' Northampton factory, Sylvia White is pictured sewing leather coats. She said: 'I'd only got to turn my head and the foreman would say, "Come on Sylvia, get your head down".' Her husband Gordon observed: 'You weren't even allowed to listen to a transistor radio, not like nowadays.' (G. White)

This is Thursday 2 June 1960 and how the media has changed, but this scene shows their enduring interest in trivia, perhaps to keep folks' minds off real problems. In this case Fyfe Robertson is asking, 'If Hercules could be brought to Northampton today, what twelve labours would you give him?' A few carefully selected answers were broadcast on the following week's 'Tonight' programme which was fronted by Cliff Michelmore and always finished with a nice song from the nice Scots duo Robin Hall and Jimmy McGregor. It also made that nice Mr Alan Whicker famous. In fact it was a very nice programme. (*Northampton Chronicle and Echo*)

H. Brain's leather shop in Harborough Road, March 1964. This shop, part of the town's old face, was about to be lost. The fading advert at the top of the dirty window tells us ironically that there is always time for a 'Cherry Blossom' shine, and at the bottom right repairs are offered, but to what? There are no more shoes here. The more modern message repeated on each of the main panes in an early example of advertising overkill says 'The Rolling Stones' are coming. (Northampton Borough Council)

The way is being cleared for a new road project from Harding Street to Monks Pond Street, April 1962. I am reminded of some words from Dominic Allard's poem 'Clearance Area':

> What proof is left
> of a hundred years
> of coming and going?
> What of the many days
> That came and went here,
> Birth and death
> Scattered among them?

(Northampton Borough Council)

The Parade was the name given to this row of buildings on the north side of the Market Square, previously known as Cornhill. This is the site of the old Emporium Arcade which housed Church's glass and china outlet, viewed from the Market Square on 12 July 1972. A campaign to save it collected 10,000 signatures and support from the National Victorian Society but to no avail. Church's was rehoused in the new Welsh House (*see* p. 107) while Abel's old-established music shop ceased trading. The corner of the old *Chronicle and Echo* building is just visible on the right. The *Northampton Mercury* was printed here from 1730 to 1978. It was redeveloped for C&A's, and the *Chronicle and Echo* has moved to The Mounts. (Northampton Borough Council)

View from the Town Wall redevelopment, 1971. Dominic Allard said: 'I was born in Kingswell Street, close to the Bassett-Lowke model-making factory. My earliest memories are of standing in the steeply sloping street, staring through the shop window at the miniature world within. The surrounding streets were a huddle of terraced housing and businesses. I also recall the sound of horses' hooves on the cobbled yard at the rear of our house. There was a dairy in Foundry Street and the cobbled yard contained the horses' stables. The yard is still there, but the rest has gone.' (Northampton Borough Council)

Sheep Street before the road widening scheme began, March 1962. So much had to change for the sake of traffic flow. (Northampton Borough Council)

Gold Street before the 'improvements', 19 May 1963. The whole area had almost been demolished in July 1941 when a crippled Stirling bomber was only just guided clear of town before its crew baled out. The plane lined itself up over Gold Street and the fuselage came down in the middle of it, ripping off the wings and scattering debris along George's Row. Luckily its bombs did not explode though one lodged on the Queen's Head Hotel – the hotel survived this but could not escape the developers in 1961 – and the doors of All Saints' Church caught fire. (Northampton Borough Council)

Market Square, June 1962. The main building here was built in 1595, and by this time had lost its original gables. It was one of the few properties to escape the great fire of 1675. People trapped by flames in the Market Square escaped through its doorways into the orchards behind. The *Northampton Herald* had offices here during the nineteenth century. In 1962 three businesses shared the premises: Nortax (left); Vanity Fayre (centre); and Ruth Tuckey (right). Just above Tuckey's is a feature incorporating the Parker family arms with an inscription in Welsh: 'Without God, without everything; with God, enough.' Samuel Parker became Bishop of Oxford in 1686. The building was rebuilt with gables in 1973 and incorporated in the Grosvenor Centre redevelopment. (Northampton Borough Council)

Lorries parked in the Mayorhold, 30 April 1962, a quaint and quiet scene which could not withstand the pressures of population growth in south-east England. The *Chronicle and Echo* reported on the bright side of the changes on 30 January 1968: 'From now on it will mean big thinking and imaginative planning so that in the words of the inquiry report, the community spirit shall not be lost.' (Northampton Borough Council)

An old Commer two-stroke lorry abandoned on derelict land off Chalk Lane, 16 August 1963. Destruction was in the air. The town already had its first three ten-storey blocks of flats at St Katherine's Court in the old Boroughs, at the expense of close-knit communities. (Northampton Borough Council)

The Christmas Prime Stock Show at the Cattle Market on 12 December 1980. There was no BSE to worry about and this 'chap's' services were much sought after. A working bull is sexually mature at 18 months. But he has a difficult sex life, either with a teaser cow which is replaced at the last moment with an artificial vagina, or with one of the latest plastic cows which looks, feels and smells like the real thing and doesn't have anything to say afterwards! A straw is half a millilitre of semen, containing around 20 million sperm. Good bulls can produce 60,000 straws a year at prices ranging from £15 to £100 per straw. (Northampton Borough Council)

Cattle Market entrance, September 1975. The market has steadily declined. Gordon Pell remembers as a boy before the war: 'I used to take cattle to market on Saturday for Mr Griffith and had to get up at five in the morning to drive the cattle down Towcester Road, along St Leonard's, over the railway level crossing and into the market; he paid me sixpence which I passed to my mum. Dad was a platelayer and that was poor pay. There were seven of us boys. It was a different world. These days they get therapy for doing bugger all.' (Northampton Borough Council)

Male unemployment is high, however much the government tinkers with statistics, and it is rising faster than among women. This impish fellow is Michael from Chiswick. He was begging outside the tourist centre when I met him last March and said: 'I have no family. I can get a bed in the hostel. I hope to win the lottery and invest in property.' So he is a man of our times in more ways than one! (R. Cook)

Claremont and Belmont flats viewed from derelict buildings in 1964. Jeremy Seabrook argued: 'It is not the slums that are being cleared from the central area so much as people. The site on which they are housed is too valuable and they must be removed. The people who came onto the streets at the end of the last century came because they had to, here were the houses and here too, on every street corner, the factories. Now, a century later, they are leaving because they have no choice. For them at least nothing has changed.' (*The Everlasting Feast*, p. 224). (Northampton Borough Council)

GIVING THE OLD TOWN A LIFT

Inside the Grosvenor Centre, 1996. (R. Cook)

Sainsbury's site in Abington Street, being cleared on 4 June 1962, as Northampton felt the first major tremors of the 1960s upheaval. But it wasn't an entirely new experience. In 1925 the Mawson Report, published by Town Planning consultants engaged by the Town Council, stated: 'Northampton's opportunity lies in having good foundations on which to build the new Northampton of the future.' The objective of the report was to make proposals for regulating the town's future growth in the interest of industrial efficiency, convenience and amenity. In 1966 the Minister of Housing and Local Government, Dick Crossman, directed consultants engaged on a similar task. On 3 February 1965 he announced to the House of Commons that, together with Ipswich and Peterborough, Northampton had been selected for a major expansion scheme to accommodate a planned intake of 70,000 people from London by 1981, followed by natural growth thereafter. The pattern followed the 1952 New Towns Act but ideally new legislation was needed to prescribe a working partnership between the government and local authority unit of the size and status of an all-purpose County Borough, but the urgency of the situation did not permit. Instead Crossman appointed Messrs Wilson and Womersley as agents. They had to recommend an area near or in Northampton which might be designated for major expansion. Thus the special powers of the New Towns Act could be used to overwhelm the old town centre as well as to find extra space nearby. Then came the publication of recommendations and time for objections, after which the Minister could have decided to abandon the project or proceed with or without modifications to his accepted plan. Beyond this, implementation had to be placed in the hands of a separate Development Corporation in which the Town Council had to be represented. As the plan moved forward the government minister was replaced by Mr Greenwood, who was equally inclined to cut corners. Some feared the kind of London people who would flood on to the new estates. The *Chronicle and Echo*'s City Editor, John Heffernan, commented: 'In a way planning a new town is like playing the most expensive game of musical chairs. The winners are those who get the nicest and most useful people on those chairs.' (Northampton Borough Council)

Central Northampton, looking north across the gas works, 12 December 1973. The old race course is visible at the top of the picture but the landscape is dominated by the trend towards high-rise buildings, and main roads divide the town into neat sections. Of the new road schemes, Jeremy Seabrook commented: 'The line of the new urban expressway is announced: it passes through the most densely populated area of the town and will demolish a thousand homes, the abodes of the powerless and the poor. In the central area of the town the houses are being cleared to make way for office and property developments. When challenged on the line of the road, the Chairman of the Highways Committee admitted that it had been designed to avoid the properties of the great employers of labour.' (*The Everlasting Feast*, p. 213.)

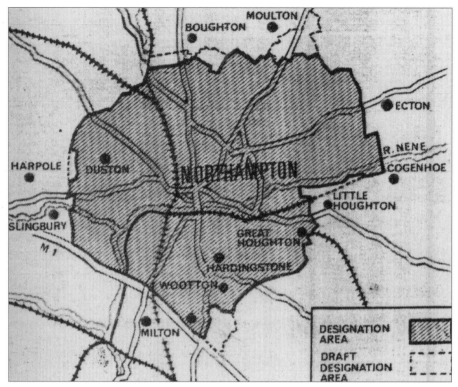

A map showing proposed developments in 1966 (*see* p. 112). Consultants Wilson and Womersley recommended an area of 35 square miles to be designated as coming under the new town. Barry Mills, looking back in May 1996, said: 'Northampton used to be a close-knit community. Alison Gardens was Northampton. That's all pulled down. It was a very poor area.' (*Northampton Chronicle and Echo*)

The road widening scheme in Welford Road, August 1962. By 1965 planners were expecting the numbers of car-owners in Northampton to quadruple, and noted that: 'A town plan must take account of a high level of car ownership and usage . . . a communications system should be designed accordingly' (*Roads in Urban Areas*, MOT). Jeremy Seabrook mused upon the subject of young mothers bringing children back from prep school in the second car and asked: 'You wonder if anything will survive in all this destructive frenzy.' (*The Everlasting Feast*, p. 208). (Northampton Borough Council)

View from the bus stop in Harborough Road, 5 March 1964. The scene includes ageing buildings, open space and simple folk. So many such vistas would soon disappear. Seabrook observed: 'When the anger of the old people being displaced did erupt, the officials displayed a pained and condescending astonishment. Had there not been exhibitions and diagrams, and maps and plans on sale to the public? Had not all the issues been publicly and exhaustively debated? Was not the master plan a legal document? They listened with distaste to the querulous belligerence of the old.' (*The Everlasting Feast*, p. 236.)

Council houses at Far Cotton, December 1973. The new estates were apparently intended to improve the lot of the poor. Let at subsidized rents and remote from old associations, they were resented by better-off homeowners and ratepayers. Some of the earlier tenants felt cut off and poorly provided for in these bleak outposts but others appreciated the facilities. (Northampton Borough Council)

Council houses at Far Cotton, December 1973, Keith Gibbins worked on Beazley's farm near here and said: 'Now there are problems: drugs, violence, burglaries. But there are some good kids and a community centre. Old Cotton used to be like a village. Now you get people from all over. I've had an interesting life – I used to be a porter at the old Angel and saw some of the stars like Danny LaRue. They were just ordinary sorts, no airs or graces.' (Northampton Borough Council)

Council housing at Far Cotton, December 1973. Motor cars are starting to fill up roads that weren't built with motorists in mind, hence there were no drives or garages. Lock-ups were eventually provided on adjacent land and some early critics of these estates argued that if people could afford cars, why should they have subsidized rents. Car owners belonged in the more prosperous middle-class suburbs, it seemed. Some also argued that the rise of suburbia killed off the spontaneous culture of the poor; people now waited on leads and cues from television and advertising. Suburbia was part of what Jeremy Seabrook called the 'new hedonism'. (Northampton Borough Council)

The town viewed from the Carlsberg brewery site, 26 May 1977. The gentle waters of the canalized river ripple past. The tanneries were near here long ago and the British Chrome Tanning Company was based in Grafton Street. This process suited the production of leather for mass-produced shoes. (Northampton Borough Council)

Photographed from St James retail park, a mother and child pass a gasometer frame in Towcester Road, March 1995. Jeremy Seabrook observed in 1974: 'Mothers were endlessly making feet for babies shoes . . . grief at the death of children was always mild and assuageable. Childhood was too undifferentiated a phenomenon for the loss of any individual child to have been keenly felt.' (*The Everlasting Feast*, p. 30). Not so the little mite in this picture: she is a child of the consumer age and must have rights and all she needs. (R. Cook)

Model of proposed housing for St James End, 1966. The reality was different. Gordon Pell returned from the Navy and went to live in Duston in 1948. He said: 'Some of the changes are disgusting. What was wrong with it before? People loved living next door to one another. Close as people are today, I think the ways of new town design change the way they behave. I've been reading the papers and I don't think we've got a better world.' A police spokesman commented on residents threatening to form vigilante groups on Spencer Estate: 'We are well aware of their concerns and have taken action on a number of occasions . . . people should not even consider taking things into their own hands because it's never the right course of action.' But it's not easy to believe in an area where Roger Conroy, chairman of the estate's residents association, claims that many people are afraid to walk down the street even in daylight. (Northampton Borough Council)

A model of the Guildhall extension scheme, 7 November 1962. (Northampton Borough Council)

Members of Northampton Development Corporation, August 1966. Their map, with all its sectors neatly marked out, looks more like a battle plan. The emphasis was on prosperity, better amenities and civic pride. Not much was made of London overspill. 'When it was realized that we were to receive Londoners, we rummaged around in folk memory and recalled our most recent contact with the inhabitants of that city, the evacuees characterized by a love of shellfish, late hours, sketchy meals void of nutrients, noisy enjoyment of life. Expansion, it was felt, meant an influx of verminous heads and petty criminals.' (*The Everlasting Feast*, p. 234.)

Express Lift Company boffins checking relays at Abbey Works during the early 1950s. They look jolly decent chaps with rather quaint old equipment, rather like a dated physics master and his prize pupil. If only that was what they meant by prosperity, I'm sure the locals would have shouted, 'More, yes please.' But reality was more like Seabrook's expected new world of office workers, sandwich bars and places for girls to buy new tights and eyeliners. (Express Lift Co.)

Solid as a rock, Mansfield's Barry Road shoe factory, which became part of Burlingtons, pictured in 1991. This is not renovation time. The Co-op wants more parking space so it's got to come down. (G. White)

Barry Road shoe factory, 1991. The demolition team didn't intend this to happen. The scaffolding collapsed but complete disaster was prevented by a sturdy lamp-post and the prompt action of a worker who shinned up the scaffold poles and tightened a few bolts. Rummaging amongst the rubble afterwards, Gordon White found a sad memento – a copy of the *Burlington Bugle*, issue number 5, dated February 1989, which said: 'Last month we told you about showrooms we were creating at 51 Maddox Street to launch our shoes both at home and overseas. In addition we intend to use the street level and basement as a small prestigious shop to illustrate the quality of merchandise available from our factories.' (G. White)

Aerial view of central Northampton, 5 June 1974, with the Guildhall making a fine centrepiece. The town has changed greatly over the six years since the *Chronicle and Echo* had written in January 1968: 'Expansion of Northampton has been given the go-ahead under the New Towns Act with only slight cutting back in the land takeover made in the draft designation order . . . designating some 19,952 acres of land in and around the town as part of the plan to provide homes for 70,000 Londoners by 1981, increasing Northampton's population to 220,000.' There were protests. Gordon Pell, who gave up his apprenticeship with the City Press to join the Navy, settled in Duston after the war, enjoying the village atmosphere. He said: 'We put a banner across the street saying "Hands off Duston." They took no notice. Village life wasn't the same afterwards.' But the good farmland beyond was protected. The newspaper reported: 'The Minister was obviously impressed by the strength of opposition to the prospective loss of good agricultural land and this "concession" will doubtless give great satisfaction.' The editorial ended: 'If all goes well it should prove an exciting journey, particularly for the younger generation who will grow up to a new inheritance so different from the old.' (Northampton Borough Council)

Northampton House dominates the skyline in the central area, 18 July 1972. In the foreground are humble flats for those fortunate enough not to be on the lengthening housing queues. (Northampton Borough Council)

A view from the new flats on the edge of the central area, July 1972. Jeremy Seabrook observed: 'As the people leave, the town centre becomes a place of windy corners and waste paper, left after 6 o'clock to the competitive patrol of guard dogs and the predatory young; and for no other reason than it is the location of employment: precisely that which has the least reason for usurping the central area which used to be our living space.' (*The Everlasting Feast*, p. 237.) (Northampton Borough Council)

Northampton House rises hideously close to the old Fancier's Working Men's Club in Wood Street, photographed on 18 July 1972. The twelve-storey building was completed at a cost of £12 million. People used to work at machines, but now they work in them as the system drives for ever more efficiency. Each window marks a new cubicle space and inside will soon be the teams and terminals connected down the wires and through the ether to the ever expanding world economy and the global village. (Northampton Borough Council)

Market Square, 1970. Country folk used to bring their surplus produce here for sale until the great watershed of the Second World War which moved people around the country, and advanced technology and outlooks almost overnight. So much was swept away from these old cobbled streets. Gordon White's grandparents told him that there used to be a dentist's tent in the market. A drum was beaten as each tooth was pulled to drown out the screams. Progress isn't all bad! (Northampton Borough Council)

The central clearance area, July 1972. The Church of the Holy Sepulchre pierces the background sky. Hard lives were lived on these disappearing streets. Why mourn them? While folk struggled for a basic existence, they had less time to be bored or disruptive or jealous. Harry Smith's mother was widowed at 28, but brought up three boys and saw them off to war. Harry never forgot to send his mother 5s a week from his Navy pay. (Northampton Borough Council)

As Northampton House rises monstrously on the right of this picture a new pattern of streets is imposed upon the central area. But the old is not quite obliterated. There are a few reminders of what it used to look like. But old thoughts and feelings are more tenuous. Jeremy Seabrook: 'Northampton society used to be old country town gentility – lawyers, doctors. They used to turn up their noses at people in trade . . . they've mostly died out now. Society is based on money and the things it can buy.' (*The Everlasting Feast*, p. 207.) (Northampton Borough Council)

Professor Frank Dobson's statue 'Woman with Fish' shortly after its unveiling in Memorial Square in May 1952. Maybe the name and the image offended feminists, even though it was probably meant to be modern enough to be all things to all people. Whatever the reason, it was daubed with paint and the head knocked off. Repaired, and after a period in hiding, it was unveiled again in the wilds of Delapre Park. (Express Lift Co.)

Britons spent £17 billion eating out in 1995 (*Euromonitor*), partly owing to the decline of the traditional family dinner. Diners like this one off St Leonard's Road use themes to grab attention. In this case it's a pink American car on the roof. Themes bring in the eaters. 'Buddies' became famous for school-uniformed waitresses. Is there a lesson in all this? I suppose that depends on the pupil! (R. Cook)

ACKNOWLEDGEMENTS

Finding room for enough words to thank all those who helped me with this project is impossible. In the first instance I am grateful to writers such as Alan Burman and Jeremy Seabrook whose work did so much to inspire my interest in the town's past and present. Jeremy Seabrook was incredibly generous in allowing me to quote so freely from his vital work, *The Everlasting Feast*. As far as writing upon Northampton's history is concerned, there have been some hard acts to follow and I hope that I have made a worthwhile contribution to the record. If there is any note of gloom it is more about the times we live in than the town itself. Those who have helped me have been patient and considerate and if they are typical of the town then it can't be at all bad. I am grateful to Brian Hensman of the Museum for encouraging me at the outset and introducing me to Gordon White. Suzanne and Terry Tarpley pointed me along some interesting highways and went out of their way to help and advise. But it seems wrong to single out individuals because however large or small the contribution it was very important. However, I must make special mention of the *Chronicle and Echo*, the ultimate recorder of the town's daily life for so long.

In some cases the extent of individual contributions is apparent from the text but I have listed their names alphabetically below. Every reasonable effort has been made to trace photograph copyright holders.

Dominic Allard • B. Barton • F. Bateman • G. Blane • M. Blane • Pip Brimson
Dr W.E. Brocklehurst • C. Butt • G. Butt • Church & Co. • S. Collier
Cosworth Engineering Ltd • N.G. Cook • N.J. Cook • M. Cousins • Express Lift Co.
K. Gibbins • M. Gibson • B. Hensman • C.A. Hodgkinson • R. Jellis
I.M. Kennedy • L. Miller • Northamptonshire Borough Council
Northamptonshire Business Link • *Northampton Chronicle and Echo*
Northants C.C. Education & Libraries • Northants FA • Northants Fire & Rescue
Northants Royal Navy & Royal Marines Association • Northampton Machinery Co.
Northants Record Office • J. Ounsworth • R. Patrick • G. Pell • Baden Powell
Sinead Ryan • J. Seabrook • L.R. Smart • W.H. Smith • Colin Stacey • S. Tarpley
T. Tarpley • British Timken • J. Walker • G. White • N. White • S. White
D.E. Wilson • J. Wooding

BRITAIN IN OLD PHOTOGRAPHS

To order any of these titles please telephone our distributor, Littlehampton Book Services on 01903 72159(

For a catalogue of these and our other titles please ring Regina Schinner on 01453 731114